JOHN MEAD

Y0-BRE-100

How To Build
Adobe Houses . . . etc.

Other TAB books by the author:

No. 2262   *How the Air Traffic Control System Works*
No. 2266   *Night Flying in Single-Engine Airplanes*
No. 2274   *The Illustrated Encyclopedia of General Aviation*

No. 1147
$12.95

How To Build Adobe Houses . . . etc.

by Paul Garrison

TAB BOOKS
BLUE RIDGE SUMMIT, PA. 17214

FIRST EDITION

FIRST PRINTING—SEPTEMBER 1979

Copyright © 1979 by TAB BOOKS

Printed in the United States of America

Reproduction or publication of the content in any manner, without express permission of the publisher, is prohibited. No liability is assumed with respect to the use of the information herein.

Library of Congress Cataloging in Publication Data

Garrison, Paul.
    How to build adobe houses.

    Bibliography: p.
    Includes index.
    1. Building, Adobe. 2. Adobe houses. I. Title.
TH4818.A3G37   693.2'2   79-17293
ISBN 0-6306-9755-1
ISBN 0-6306-1147-9 pbk.

ISBN 0-8306-9755-1
ISBN 0-8306-1147-9 pbk.

Contents

Introduction

This book is not intended to miraculously transform the reader into a first-rate architect or an efficient contractor. Rather it will deal with the inherent beauty and flexibility of adobe as a building material which, to a much greater degree than any other such material, permits individual artistic expression in the planning and execution of a home or structure, while reducing the need to deal with such hard-to-handle modern building materials as steel and cement.

The potential adobe builder should think of himself as a sculptor designing a three-dimensional work of art which, incidentally, is also intended to serve as a comfortable dwelling for himself and his family. He will, of course, have to remember that it must include such prosaic necessities as bathrooms, kitchens, means of providing heat and ventilation, closets, storage space and so on. But all of these are part and parcel of any structure intended for human habitation and should in no way inhibit the degree of artistic expression used in the design of the basic exterior shape.

What this book will try to do is to dwell on the excitement of adobe building. There are endless possibilities in terms of form and shape which can and should be a delight to the eye when approached from any direction under all conceivable light conditions. There are chapters on the basic techniques involved in working with adobe, but the serious builder who will get his hands dirty and turn his dream sculpture into reality should get advice and help from men experienced in the actual back-breaking job of doing the real building. Advance research and listening to the experiences of others will prevent getting caught in time consuming and often costly mistakes. It will also help give the do-it-yourself builder a reasonably accurate estimate as to the amount of time and money he will have to devote to the project.

No matter how ambitious the builder, and no matter how outwardly simple the project to be built, the amateur architect-contractor is bound to overlook necessary and important details. He is likely to make mistakes in the consecutive order in which each individual task should be started and completed. He is likely to be overly optimistic with regard to the amount of time needed which tends to run from 2,000 to 3,000 man hours even for those who are skilled in the trade. Probably more than twice that amount will be needed for anyone undertaking such a job for the first time and planning to use the absolute minimum of expert and paid assistance.

While a detailed analysis of all the myriad of tasks involved may cause the project as a whole to appear staggering, it is, in fact, simply a large succession of small jobs. Each of them is a minor achievement, eventually adding up to the envisioned whole.

But enough of all this talk of time and money and aching muscles or calloused hands. Let's look at adobe itself, its history, its beauty and the visual excitement which it is capable of at the hands of a talented designer.

That, then, is one part of the purpose of this book. The other is to serve as a primer for amateur builders.

Paul Garrison

Chapter 1
What Is Adobe?

The word itself is commonly used to denote a number of different meanings. It stands for the clayey soil which, when appropriately treated, turns into a hard and weather resistant building material. It stands for the buildings made from this material and in some cases for structures made from other materials but conforming to what is generally referred to as the adobe style. And it also is used to describe the individual bricks made from dried adobe soil and constituting the primary structural ingredient in most adobe buildings (Fig. 1-1).

It is of a somewhat uncertain origin, described by Webster as having derived from the Arabic *at-tub* and the Coptic *tobe*, both meaning brick. On the other hand, the *Encyclopedia Britannica* claims it to be a derivative of the Spanish word *adobar*, meaning to plaster.

But be that as it may, adobe is simply plain ordinary mud, found in most of the more arid regions of the globe, consisting in varying proportions of clay, sand and a variety of organic matter. When mixed with water and subsequently dried it turns rock hard, though frequent exposure to excessive amount of moisture may cause it eventually to crumble and subsequently disintegrate (Fig. 1-2).

Primitive peoples, finding it readily available underfoot and easier to work with than lumber or rock with their simple or often no tools, started to use it thousands of years ago to build uncomplicated conical or round mudhuts as protection against the elements and enemies.

Fig. 1-1. Adobe bricks, made from adobe mud and sun-dried, are the primary building material in most adobe buildings.

Today, in many areas where the appropriate soil is readily available, adobe can be commercially purchased, usually in the form of adobe bricks. It is widely used in combination with lumber, cement blocks and other materials which permit maintaining its esthetic advantages (Fig. 1-3) while minimizing the detrimental qualities with reference to permanence. This is especially true in locations where frequent precipitation or sub-freezing temperatures would otherwise result in the need for frequent and annoying repairs.

Not everyone finds the adobe look pleasing (Fig. 1-4). It does not readily lend itself to the so-called California ranch-style houses with their immense expanse of picture windows and sliding glass doors (Figs. 1-5 through 1-8). Similarly no one in his right mind would think of using adobe to build a New England *saltbox*, and it is certainly not the ideal material for a high-rise structure, the multi-storied adobe "apartment house" at the Taos Pueblo in New Mexico not withstanding.

It is ideal for the single-family dwelling which will, if designed and constructed with love and the eye of an artist, look like no other anywhere and be one of a kind—a monument expressing the taste of its creator (Fig. 1-9).

Fig. 1-2. Adobe needs protection and constant attention. When left indefinitely exposed to moisture it will gradually disintegrate.

Fig. 1-3. Adobe, to a greater degree than any other building material, permits individual artistic expression in the planning and execution of a home.

13

Fig. 1-5. This home along the Camino del Monte Sol in Santa Fe maintains the typical adobe character.

Fig. 1-6. Older adobe homes such as this one often include carved wooden doors, vigas and row wood beams for lintels above windows and garage doors.

Fig. 1-4. The adobe look does not appeal to everyone.

Fig. 1-7. This home includes the typical adobe characteristic of rounded surfaces rather than sharp corners.

Fig. 1-8. Adobe walls often surround the property of an adobe home.

16

Fig. 1-9. Adobe offers endless possibilities in terms of form and shape which delight the eye when approached from any direction under varying light conditions.

17

Fig. 1-10. A carefully sculpted adobe wall encircles a small front patio in the front of a home on Camino del Monte Sol in Santa Fe.

Adobe means no sharp corners and no glass-smooth flat planes. It lends itself to all manner of sweeping curves, meandering lines and walls with just a sufficient suggestion of topography to catch the light (Fig. 1-10).

In the old days, when it was used without the addition of strengthening materials, it often resulted in massive structures with three or four-foot-thick walls and immense exterior buttresses blending into the outer surfaces. Then its superior insulating qualities kept outdoor cold and heat from seeping into the interior. Windows were kept small and doors to a minimum. Few examples of this kind of construction remain today with the possible exception of some of the more exciting churches erected by the Spaniards during the time of their occupation of much of the southwestern United States (Figs. 1-11 and 1-12).

HISTORY OF ADOBE

And that brings us to the history of adobe architecture in North America as originated by the Pueblo Indians many centuries before Columbus conned Queen Isabella into financing his westward trip to what he expected to be India; to the subsequent influence on style and construction by the Spanish conquerers and missionaries; and to the changes wrought by the gradual introduction of a variety of additional building materials and the acceptance of more modern construction methods.

Fig. 1-11. An excellent example of the massive building style often used in the construction of churches by the Spanish missionaries with the help of their Indian converts. This church is located near the Nambe Pueblo north of Santa Fe.

Fig. 1-12. The side view of the church in Nambe Pueblo shows how abutments have been built into the thick walls to give them extra strength. The canales stick out several feet from the roof to prevent draining rain water or melting snow from running down the side of the walls and impairing the adobe plaster.

ADOBE RELICS

The oldest remaining adobe structures in North America are the ruins (Fig. 1-13) of extremely complicated and apparently highly sophisticated Indian settlements, whose occupants, for no known reason, either died out or simply abandoned their homes to go elsewhere some two thousand years ago. No one knows where they went.

Chaco Canyon National Monument, an area of some 16 square miles in northwestern New Mexico, contains the ruins of thirteen great pueblos plus several hundred smaller ones, most said to date back to around 500 A.D., the time when the Anasazi Indians are said to have gradually relinquished their earlier nomadic existence in favor of agriculture and communal living. Using a combination of native rock and adobe, they built immense structures, housing the entire tribe in what was, in fact, one continuous building (Fig. 1-14). Of those in the Chaco Canyon area, Pueblo Bonito is the most famous and best preserved. Once, centuries ago, it rose five stories high, covered more than three acres and contained close to a thousand rooms including 34 kivas, circular ceremonial chambers devoted to religious functions.

What caused these people to one day simply walk away from their cities is not known. What is known is the fact that during the thirteenth century there was a period of little rain and prolonged drought, and other Indian tribes, those known today as the Apaches

Fig. 1-13. An aerial view of the ruins of the nearly 2,000 year old pueblos at Canyon National Monument, considered the cradle of the Indian pueblo civilization.

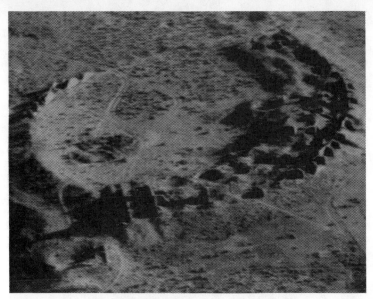

Fig. 1-14. More ruins of the nearly 2,000 year old Indian pueblos.

and Navajos, attracted by the apparent wealth of the Anasazi began raiding the pueblos for food. They were later renamed Pueblo Indians by the Spaniards—the Spanish word *pueblo* meaning town or village.

Fig. 1-15. A typical structure of the mesa built atop an outcropping against the side of the cliffs.

The Puebloans, in turn, searched for safer places in which to live, places which could more successfully be defended. Today the entire Four Corners area—the place where Arizona, Colorado, New Mexico and Utah meet—is dotted with cliff dwellings and intricate rock and adobe structures built into the near-vertical sides of sandstone cliffs and atop virtually inaccessible mesas. The best known among them are those at Puye Cliffs and in Bandelier National Monument, both near Santa Fe, New Mexico; in Mesa Verde National Park in southwestern Colorado; and in the still inhabited Acoma Pueblo, known as the Sky City, some 60 miles west of Albuquerque. Some miles west of Espanola in northern New Mexico the mesa known as Puye Cliffs rises steeply out of the surrounding terrain (Figs. 1-15 through 1-19). In centuries past, the forebearers of today's Santa Clara Pueblo Indians built veritable fortresses against and into the sides of the cliffs as a means of protection against roving nomadic Indian tribes and, in later years, the conquering Spaniards and Anglos. Using adobe bricks they constructed multi-storied dwellings, using vigas to separate the stories and to support the adobe roofs. The vigas were at one end, set into the relatively soft rock. Depending on the length used, they were left sticking out of the walls on the other end. Ladders were used to climb from one level to the next. They were pulled up in the event of an enemy attack. Figure 1-15 shows a typical two-story structure built atop an outcropping against the side of the cliffs. In Figure 1-16 you can

Fig. 1-16. Cliff dwellings are practically inaccessible. Note the top of a ladder at the far left leading into a natural cave.

Fig. 1-17. Some structures were built between natural rocks and were partially supported by them.

visualize the inaccessability of such cliff dwellings. The top of a ladder at the far left leads into a natural cave. Figure 1-17 shows a tall, narrow adobe brick structure built between natural rocks and partially supported by them. Note the round holes in the cliffs above which once held vigas for long-ago disintegrated dwellings. In Figure 1-18 all that is left to indicate past inhabitation is a ladder, leading from one narrow ledge to another. Again you can see the round holes which once upon a time supported vigas. The typical remains of what once was a sizeable cliff dwelling are seen in Figure 1-19. You can clearly see by the viga holes where the outer buildings stood in front of an entire series of natural caves.

This mesa originally had no natural access from the surrounding areas. Today a somewhat precipitous road leads to the top, making it possible to drive up. An acre or more is covered with the ruins of what once must have been a veritable adobe city. Stripped of the protecting plaster by centuries of weather, the adobe bricks show where hundreds of rooms housed the Peublo Indians (Fig. 1-20). Several circular kivas were excavated and constructed underground. Some are still in fair shape. Among the rubble there still

Fig. 1-18. A ladder led from one narrow ledge to another.

remains a two-story structure, bearing witness to the fact that this was once a multi-story peublo (Fig. 1-21).

Though each of today's pueblos represents an independent tribe with its own individual language or dialect, they do all share a mutual history and tradition. Thus it is easy to see why the architectural styles, having survived to this day, are of common imagery and methods of construction (Figs. 1-22 through 1-25). They have rounded corners, flat roofs serving as terraces for upper stories and rough-hewn outdoor ladders instead of indoor stairs. The rooms themselves are small with ceilings of vigas and latillas supporting the roof. Small corner fireplaces provide a degree of warmth during the long New Mexico winters.

In Indian tradition applying the outer finish to a dwelling was the work of the women. Close examination of the sculptured walls often still shows where loving female hands smoothed the adobe surface (Fig. 1-26). It is this peculiar characteristic of adobe—the fact that it permits itself to be shaped and formed by hand rather than inanimate tools—which gives it its unique appearance.

While much of what we think of today as adobe architecture is derived from the work of the North American Indians, adobe is by no means exclusive to this part of the world. It has been and still is widely used in some of the more arid regions of Africa where the

Dogon people of Mali used adobe to sculpt incredibly intricate temples. Farther north the Arabs used it to build entire towns and villages, many of them strikingly similar in style to those of the Indians. Mexico, too, as well as Central and South America are dotted with fine examples of using adobe in combination with native rock and other conveniently available matter as building material.

There are entire adobe cities in India and as far away as China. The famous lamaseries in Tibet are built of adobe. As a matter of fact, historians who have made a study of the subject claim that to this day close to half the population of the entire world is living in adobe-type structures.

As far as North America is concerned, it is only logical that with the arrival of the white man in the new world, the traditional style of Indian architecture underwent much adjustment and change.

For over three hundred years, from 1539 to 1848, much of the southwestern United States was either under Spanish occupation or a part of Mexico. Thus the Spaniards exerted a strong, and to some degree lasting, influence on architectural styles. Much of it is due to the individual desire to express personal success and wealth through magnificent mansions. This was an idea which had been entirely foreign to the Indian culture which believed that each being was as an

Fig. 1-19. Typical remains of cliff dwellings.

Fig. 1-20. Adobe bricks show where hundreds of rooms housed Pueblo Indians at this mesa.

integral part of the overall environment with neither right nor desire for land ownership or personal possession.

MONUMENTAL ADOBE BUILDINGS

Adobe did continue to be the primary building material, and in the early days of the Spanish occupation the basic Indian style was reasonably faithfully followed. One good example of this includes the Government Palace in Santa Fe, built entirely of adobe in 1609. It is the oldest public building in the United States. Erected atop an old pueblo, it incorporates some of its original walls in its structure (Figs. 1-27 through 1-29).

Another example is the so-called Oldest House, also in Santa Fe (Figs. 1-30 and 1-31).

The many churches built by Spanish missionaries with Indian labor offer more examples. Buttresses of adobe and rock were built to strengthen the walls of the San Miguel in Santa Fe (Fig. 1-32). This church is considered to be the oldest church in the United States.

Some of the most magnificent examples include the church at Racho de Taos (Figs. 1-33 and 1-34) and the massive adobe church at Nambe, New Mexico (Fig. 1-35).

Fig. 1-21. Among the rubble of this mesa, there still remains a two story structure.

Fig. 1-22. The multi-story Indian pueblo near Taos, New Mexico. This pueblo is known to have been continuously inhabited for over 700 years. It is still in regular use today.

Fig. 1-23. Another view of an Indian pueblo in New Mexico that is still in use today.

Fig. 1-24. Flat roofs serve as terraces for the upper stories of this Indian pueblo.

Fig. 1-25. Indian pueblos used rough-hewn outdoor ladders instead of indoor stairs.

Fig. 1-26. The outer finish of a dwelling was usually smoothed by the hands of women.

Fig. 1-27. The oldest public building in the United States is the Governor's Palace in Santa Fe.

Fig. 1-28. The Governor's Palace in Santa Fe was built in 1609 atop an old Indian pueblo.

Fig. 1-29. Some of its old walls are still incorporated in the structure of the Governor's Palace in Santa Fe.

Fig. 1-30. This very old adobe in Santa Fe is claimed to be the oldest house in the United States.

Fig. 1-31. This so-called oldest house in the United States is often visited by tourists in Santa Fe.

Fig. 1-32. The San Miguel Church in Santa Fe is considered to be the oldest church in the United States.

Fig. 1-33. A magnificent example of adobe architecture includes the church at Taos Pueblo.

The Santuario de Chimayo which is halfway between Santa Fe and Taos in northern New Mexico is one of the finer examples of early Spanish use of adobe in church construction (Fig. 1-36). Facing a cemetery surrounded by an adobe wall with a beautiful old wooden gate (Fig. 1-37), the Santuario is built atop a place where the earth is

Fig. 1-34. The adobe church at Taos Pueblo has recently been restored.

Fig. 1-35. The adobe church at Nambe, New Mexico is massive.

said to have miraculous healing qualities. An opening in the floor inside the church permits worshippers to dig up small quantities of this earth which is then used in order to try to cure a number of ailments.

Fig. 1-36. This old Spanish adobe church is still in regular use today.

Fig. 1-37. The Sanctuario de Chimayo faces a cemetery surrounded by an adobe wall with this beautiful old wooden gate.

Fig. 1-38. The construction of this church at Las Trampas included massive walls.

Fig. 1-39. A close look at the turret of the church at Las Trampas shows the deteriorating effects of weather.

Figures 1-38 through 1-41 are four views of the church at Las Trampas, located on a back road leading from Santa Fe to Taos. The massive walls, thickened further by repeated applications of more and more plaster, in their not quite straight lines bear witness to hand work done over the years. A close look at the turrets shows the deteriorating effects of weather and the impending need for one more coat of plaster. Wood was used effectively to create simple but pleasing designs. As is typical of most of the churches of that period, this one is also surrounded by an adobe wall with a wooden gate.

Fig. 1-40. Wood was used to create simple but pleasing designs on the adobe church at Las Trampas.

El Cristo Rey, located on Canyon Road in Santa Fe, is said to be one of the largest adobe structures of its kind. Awe-inspiring in its massive simplicity (Fig. 1-42), it bears witness to the beauty of line, lights and shade which is one of the unique qualities of building with adobe. The covered walk to the rear door of the church uses raw vigas to support an adobe-mud roof, using flat lumber in a herringbone design as decking (Figs. 1-43 and 1-44).

An elegantly carved front door brings you inside (Fig. 1-45). The interior of the El Cristo Rey church combines simplicity of form with intricate wood carvings. The high viga and latilla ceiling with its handcarved corbels on either side helps to effect the hushed quiet which we expect of a church interior (Fig. 1-46). An early Spanish handcarved crucifix is the sole decoration on one of the walls inside El Cristo Rey (Fig. 1-47).

Also included here should be the monumental church at Acoma (Figs. 1-48 and 1-49), not because of any particular architectural distinction but because it seems quite incredible to us today how its builders were able to bring the huge quantities of building material up that torturous crevice which served as the only means of getting from the valley floor to the top of the mesa. The torturous narrow path was the only access to the Acoma Pueblo atop the mesa in the old days (Figs. 1-50 through 1-53). All materials to build the huge church as well as the dwellings had to be carried by hand up this path.

Fig. 1-41. The church at Las Trampas was surrounded by an adobe wall with a wooden gate.

Fig. 1-42. El Cristo Rey is awe-inspiring in its massive simplicity.

Fig. 1-45. The elegantly carved front door to the Cristo Rey Church.

A final example is the Fine Arts Museum on Palace Avenue in Santa Fe, generally considered one of the finest examples of the use of adobe in a public building (Figs. 1-54 and 1-55). In order to maintain its beauty and structural integrity it, too, needs frequent attention. On the shaded part of the wall in the center of the

Fig. 1-43. A covered walk brings you to the rear door of El Cristo Rey.

Fig. 1-44. Flat lumber is used in a herringbone design as decking for this adobe church.

Fig. 1-46. The interior of the El Cristo Rey church combines simplicity of form with intricate wood carvings.

photograph of Figure 1-54 we can see where a section of plaster has weathered away, and will soon have to be repaired in order to prevent water from seeping into the walls themselves.

MODERN ADOBE DWELLINGS

As time passed tools began to replace human hands and the pleasantly rounded surfaces of the older adobes were replaced by sharp corners. Instead of vigas throwing their slanted shadows across the walls, roof edges were lined with fired red brick, arranged

Fig. 1-48. This immense adobe and rock church is at the Acoma Pueblo.

Fig. 1-49. The Acoma Pueblo church turret.

Fig. 1-47. An early Spanish crucifix decorates El Cristo Rey.

in all manner of intricate designs. Thus a style was born which still remains popular today, known as *Territorial* (Figs. 56 and 57). Though originally also built primarily of adobe, its basic character had been lost and by now few would think of using that word with reference to a territorial home.

By now, with the continuing migration of people from all parts of the country to the Southwest, things seem to be coming full circle. Brand new homes are being built in large numbers by amateurs and professionals (Fig. 1-58) not only using adobe as the primary building

Fig. 1-50. This narrow path led to Acoma Pueblo.

material (Fig. 1-59), but also closely imitating the style of the traditional Indian dwelling.

An example of an older Indian dwelling is found in Figure 1-60. This small corner deep inside the Taos Pueblo illustrates how each room or group of rooms opens onto a small outdoor balcony. During

Fig. 1-51. At one time the only access to Acoma Pueblo was by this tortuous path.

the warmer seasons the balcony serves as the primary living area. There are no indoor stairs, therefore ladders are everywhere, providing access to the upper stories. In centuries past they provided protection from enemies since the ladders could be pulled up, making assault on the inhabitants of the pueblo difficult. The adobe-clad chimneys bear witness to the profusion of fireplaces inside. Through the opening between the two walls at the bottom we see a corner of a *horno*, still used today for the purpose of baking bread.

Fig. 1-52. Huge quantities of building material were carried up this path to build Acoma Pueblo atop the mesa.

Modern adobe buildings naturally vary from the original designs slightly. The rooms are now large and there are more and bigger windows. Also, instead of outdoor ladders, indoor staircases lead to upper stories. Poured cement or cement blocks are used for foundations, and in many instances lumber is incorporated with the adobe bricks in the construction of walls. But both inside and out most builders use much care to do away with sharp corners and angles, replacing them with the pleasantly rounded sculptured look of the ancient adobes (Fig. 1-61).

Fig. 1-53. Hand and footholds are worn into the rock from generations of use.

Figures 1-62 through 1-65 are perfect examples of how modern architects and builders have been able to adapt modern building materials to reproduce the traditional adobe style with a considerable degree of faithfulness. Figure 1-62 shows the multi-story Taos Pueblo, which is known to have been continuously used as living quarters by the Taos Pueblo Indians for over seven centuries, dating

Fig. 1-54. The Fine Arts Museum in Santa Fe is generally considered one of the finest examples of the use of adobe in a public building.

Fig. 1-55. Intricate carving distinguishes the balcony above the front entrance to the Fine Arts Museum.

47

Fig. 1-56. The Sena Plaza in Santa Fe is one of the more outstanding examples of the Territorial style of building with adobe. Note the intricate brickwork along the roof.

Fig. 1-57. A modern home which copies the traditional Territorial style.

Fig. 1-58. New adobe homes are being built by amateurs and professionals.

Fig. 1-59. Many new homes are using adobe as the primary building material.

49

Fig. 1-60. Groups of rooms upon rooms are remnants of old Indian adobe dwellings.

Fig. 1-61. Liberal use of adobe permits the builder considerable liberty in the design of an individual home, as is obvious in this large hillside dwelling being built north of Santa Fe.

50

Fig. 1-62. The multi-story Taos Pueblo has been kept in excellent repair by the Indians.

back to the thirteenth century or possibly earlier. Rising in places up to five stories, it has been kept in excellent repair by the Indians by constantly replastering the walls to replace the adobe washed away by rain and melting snow.

Fig. 1-63. A brand new condominium complex, built to resemble the adobe style, is actually constructed of conventional concrete block, lath and plaster.

Fig. 1-64. A modern adobe style condominium complex can be found in New Mexico.

Even commercial buildings, hotels, apartment houses and condominiums, though, in fact using little or no adobe in the construction, are painstakingly finished to look like traditional adobes (Figs. 1-63 and 1-64).

Figure 1-65 is of the newest, most elegant, most expensive hotel in Santa Fe, the Inn at the Loretto. Built in 1974 and 1975, it is constructed of concrete, lathband plaster, rises to four stories (the maximum permitted in Santa Fe) and carefully copies the traditional Indian style. In Santa Fe, the Historical Society has been eminently successful in maintaining a pleasing harmony of architectural style

Fig. 1-65. A new and elegant hotel in Santa Fe is constructed of concrete and lathband plaster.

Chapter 2

Doodles Of Your Adobe Home

Bill Lear, the famous designer of airplanes and inventor of the car radio, eight track stereo and a great variety of other electronic marvels, once said that the most important part in designing anything is the time spent doodling. "You do a good job doodling, and chances are you'll come up with a good design."

While, at the time, he was talking about designing an airplane, the advice is just as valid when it comes to designing a home.

From the moment you first start thinking in terms of building a new home, it's a good idea to keep a pencil and paper handy to write down anything that comes to mind that might be a desirable feature. The number of bedrooms, guest rooms, full, three-quarter or half baths, living room, dining area, den, closets, work room, storage space, entry hall, pantry, the size and kind of kitchen, patios and other outdoor areas such as balconies or verandahs, garage or carport, flower gardens, lawns, etc. The list of things which may be important to one person and meaningless to another is endless.

DOODLING IN FUTURE TERMS

Think not only in terms of today, but tomorrow and five and ten years from now. Today's young children soon grow into teenagers and young adults with different needs. You aren't going to get any younger either and steps which may be fine today could turn into a chore a decade from now.

Think in terms of convenience. Can the groceries be unloaded from the car and brought into the house on a rainy day without you and them getting soaked? Are there going to be enough closets not only for clothes, coats and hats, but for linens, for liquor, and above all for all the junk that tends to accumulate over the years while a house is being lived in?

With all of this in mind, start to doodle. For this you don't need a ruler and you don't have to worry about exact measurements. Just make rough drawings. Don't be satisfied with the first, second or even third. Make dozens, hundreds. The more you doodle, the clearer a picture you'll start to get in your head as to the kind of house that would really be right for you and your family.

PERFECTING YOUR DOODLES

When you think you've got something that feels right, then is the time to get a ruler. Buy yourself an architect's scale and use it to transpose the result of your doodling into an actual plan. Use a scale of a ¼ inch to 1 foot and you'll be able to get a plan for the entire house and its surroundings on one reasonably sized sheet of paper.

The Basics

Certain basics must be kept in mind. No room should be wider than 20 feet regardless of length, or structural problems will develop. The smallest bathroom size for a full bath, including the tub, sink, and toilet, is about 8 by 5 feet. Standard tubs measure 5 feet and nonstandard tubs, whether larger or smaller, tend to cost nearly twice as much. Closets for clothes should be 2 feet deep, hallways should not be narrower than 3 feet and standard kitchen counter tops are 25 inches wide. Standard doors are 30 inches wide. But remember, appliances and large furniture will have to be brought into the house; and the doors the larger pieces will come through must be of adequate size. If stairs are involved, each step should be not less than 7 and not more than 8 inches high. They should be 10 inches deep. If you have or plan to buy oversized pieces of furniture or a larger than normal refrigerator or freezer, be sure to allow for the space needed to accommodate them.

Grouping Rooms

Where possible, keep in mind that it saves money to group rooms which require plumbing in relative proximity to one another, but don't ruin the whole plan with such considerations. A few hundred dollars spent on extra plumbing is going to be a drop in the bucket in the overall scheme of things.

Fig. 2-1. Windows in a restored old adobe catch the rays of the setting sun and offer an always exciting view of the ever-changing sunsets.

Orientation

Think in terms of orientation. Some rooms will receive the morning sun, some the evening sun and some will have a view (Fig. 2-1). It would be foolish to have the morning sun hit the garage and the best view outside a guest room window.

Separation of Activities

Think in terms of separation of activities. You may want the children's area, which usually means clutter and noise, separated from the rest of the house. Will it be possible to contain the smell of cooking in the kitchen area or will it permeate the entire place? Do you enjoy eating outdoors and, if so, is it going to be easy to take the food out to the patio without dragging it all across the living room rug?

FLOOR PLAN

The overall floor plan may, of course, vary considerably with the size of your lot, your own personal preferences and, last but by no means least, the amount of money you can afford to spend. In days past, when settlers had to worry about protecting themselves and their families from the dangers associated with the absence of law enforcement as we know it today, many homes took on the character of a veritable fortress. The house would be built like a rectangular wall of rooms around a large patio with only one entrance, large enough to admit horses, wagons and livestock. Outside

Fig. 2-2. The Sena Plaza, originally a family home built around a large rectangular patio, today houses stores, offices and a restaurant.

windows were kept to a minimum and all family living took place within the confines of the house and patio. An excellent and rather spectacular example of this type of home is the Sena Plaza in Santa Fe (Fig. 2-2). Today, instead of being a family home, it houses a variety of stores, offices and a restaurant. Another is the Governor's Palace, built in the early 17th century atop an old Indian pueblo and incorporating some of the original adobe walls (Figs. 1-27, 1-28, and 1-29).

Today this kind of floor plan would be excessively wasteful in terms of space, not to mention its impracticality. Still, the idea of spreading the house over a large area may be very appealing to some people. Others prefer to think in terms of a compact unit with all rooms in close proximity to one another. An important consideration in this respect is the climate. In areas with long summers and mild winters it might be perfectly feasible to think in terms of a sleeping unit, a cooking and eating unit, a play and entertainment unit and so on. To use an extreme example, they could all be connected by covered outdoor walks. Or, alternately, several wings could be devoted to the different activities, extending from a central connecting area with individual patios between them. The overall square footage needed for such a plan may not be much greater than for one in which all rooms adjoin each other. Also, since the overall cost of construction depends largely on the total amount of square footage, it might only be slightly more expensive.

PROFESSIONAL ADVICE

In any case, whatever type of floor plan appeals to you, it would be advisable to take your ideas to a professional architect or builder, preferably the former, and discuss them at length. The past experience of such professionals is worth whatever it may cost in terms of

Fig. 2-3. Adobe lends itself to many unconventional designs and shapes.

Fig. 2-4. There are round adobe homes and oval ones and others with multi-story towers.

preventing you from making expensive and impractical mistakes.

Use their advice and knowledge with reference to practical things, such as heating, plumbing, building code requirements and so on. However, don't let them talk you out of the individuality in terms of design. Many commercial builders and some architects seem to be incapable of thinking in terms of anything except the thoroughly conventional. Faced by a lot with an unusual topography, the first thing they're likely to do is hire a bulldozer to flatten the whole thing into a characterless city lot and then put up a house that looks like a million others.

UNCONVENTIONAL DESIGNS

The whole charm of using adobe as a primary building material is that it lends itself to unconventional designs and shapes (Fig. 2-3). There are round adobe homes and oval ones (Fig. 2-4), some partially underground and others with multi-story towers. Just by driving around Santa Fe and the surrounding countryside one can find dozens of entirely different design concepts, each representing the individual taste and needs of the person or family for whom it was conceived (Fig. 2-5).

Fig. 2-5. Each adobe home represents the individual tastes of the family living in it.

Some are the expression of a desire for communal family living with privacy for the individual reduced to a minimum. They might consist of a large space with cooking, eating and living areas, but a minimum of separating walls or doors. Some will have large window areas to bring a feeling of the outside into the house, while others have reduced the size and number of windows to a minimum, preferring to shut out the outside when living indoors. Some are all on one level and in others each room is a step or two above or below the level of the next. In still others a desire for individual privacy produced a multitude of individual rooms, studios, workshops, dens and possibly separate guest houses.

This is going to be your home, and the way you design and build it is going to strongly influence you and your family's life style for years to come. The idea is to make the home fit the life style you are comfortable with. You shouldn't have to adjust your life style to the house. Otherwise you might as well buy a ready-made house and eliminate the bother of planning and building.

Chapter 3

A Little About A Lot

Wanting to build a house is one thing. Finding the right piece of land to build it on is something else. The selection of a building site is probably the most important single decision that has to be made. A house, even after it has been built, can be enlarged, renovated and even changed to some degree, but the location of the lot, its relation to the surroundings, its topography, and in most cases, its size cannot be changed.

WHERE TO BUILD

What kind of lot appeals to you is a matter of personal preference, coupled with a variety of purely practical considerations. There are nice, orderly rectangular building sites on level ground, or there are odd-shaped plots on hillsides or lots sliced in half by an arroyo which is probably dry all year except for a day or two when the melting snow turns it into a churning river.

Figure 3-1 illustrates a large hillside home under construction. A mixture of adobe, concrete blocks and lumber is being used. The walls are up, door and window openings are in place and the vigas are in place. The chimney at the right, sticking up above the yet unfurnished roof, bears witness to the location of one of several fireplaces in this building.

In the construction of the home in Fig. 3-2, which is located against a steep hillside, the concrete-block stem was built up to an unusual height since it has to double as a retaining wall. One story is more or less complete with a second story in the early stages of being built. Note the wooden pole nailed to the side of the wall to assure that the upper wall surface remains perfectly vertical.

There are other lots bordering on paved streets and others stuck away somewhere in the boondocks which require the building of a road in order to be accessible. Or it may be located on a narrow, steep road which becomes impassable during the snow season, except by means of a four-wheel drive vehicle or by using chains (Fig. 3-3). There are lots with spectacular views and others stuck in little valleys surrounded by hills or mountains. And then, of course, there are those which fall within your budget and those which you may fall in love with but can't afford.

PRACTICAL CONSIDERATIONS

First, let's look at the practical considerations. If you have school age kids, or if you and your wife must be at an office or place of business five days a week, you may prefer to think of a location reasonably close to your town or city, rather than one which involves having to drive long distances day after day.

Fig. 3-1. A large adobe home is under construction on a hillside.

Fig. 3-2. Often the concrete-block system is built up to an unusual height for homes built on a hillside.

THE NEIGHBORHOOD

If that is the case, look at the surroundings, the other homes in the area and the people who will be your immediate neighbors. Whatever you see you'll be stuck looking at for years to come because the basic looks and character of a neighborhood aren't likely to change. Also check on such things as utilities, sewers and the like. The ease or difficulty with which access to these can be achieved may make a multi-thousand-dollar difference in the cost of your home. Even the quality of television reception is a major importance to a lot of us these days.

Fig. 3-3. Some lots are located on narrow steep roads which can become virtually impassable during rain or snow seasons, except by four wheel drive vehicles.

LEGAL RESTRICTIONS

Check on easements and restrictions which affect the potential orientation of the house on the lot. There may be minimum distance requirements which would prevent you from building as close to the lot line as you would like. And be sure that the seller will guarantee a clear title. You don't want to take a chance of getting involved in some sort of legal hassle over some ancient and obscure dispute involving the lot of your choice.

Regardless of whether you want to buy close to town or miles away from the madding crowd, the following is a simple checklist of subjects to keep in mind.

Location. This includes privacy; distance from schools, markets, office, etc.; and traffic problems, if any.

Size and shape. Knowing roughly the kind and size of home you have in mind, is the lot large enough and of the shape which will permit you to build the house you are envisioning?

Surroundings. Are the surroundings to your liking? Remember that even if you are planning to enclose the entire area with an adobe wall (Fig. 3-4), you'll have to look at the surroundings every time you come or go.

Access. Is the place easy to get to, or will you have to spend a small fortune to build an access road or driveway which will remain passable under all weather conditions?

Utilities. Are water, electricity and gas readily available? Bringing in an electric line from some distant spot can cost thousands of dollars. Water is a must. If no water connection is available, are you prepared to drill a well? Do you have the right to do so? If no gas line is nearby, are you prepared to operate with LPG, and if so, is it available at an acceptable price?

Sewers or septic tanks. Is there a sewer and, if so, what will it cost to be connected to it? Will you be stuck with the cost of tearing up a portion of the pavement of the street and then having it replaced? If no sewer is available, is there adequate space somewhere on the lot to bury a septic tank and room for the associated leach field? Septic tanks do have to be pumped out from time to time, therefore there must be some kind of access for the pump truck.

Topography. Is the ground flat or on the side of a steep hill? How easy or difficult and in turn, expensive, will it be to bring all the needed building materials to the site and to pour the foundation? Will there be a need to erect retaining walls? Is the ground undisturbed and thus capable of supporting the foundation and the structure? Is there fill which would require digging deep down to get to firm ground?

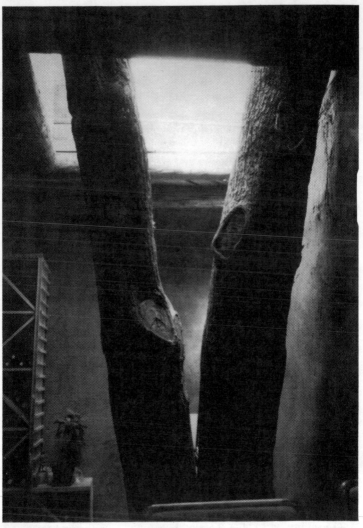

Fig. 3-5. Even if there is a tree in the way of the house, you might wish to consider building around it. This huge tree happily grows right through the dining room at the Periscope, a Santa Fe restaurant.

Trees and shrubs. Remember that it takes years for trees and shrubs to grow to any respectable size. Any greenery which isn't in the way of the actual house should be left undisturbed. Most commercial builders seem to love to totally denude a building site, resulting in houses sitting sort of naked on an ugly piece of bare earth. It is often worthwhile when planning the house to keep in mind existing vegetation and to take full advantage of it.

Fig. 3-4. An adobe wall offers privacy for the inhabitants of this small adobe home.

Legalities. Deal with a reputable real estate agent and a lawyer. Be sure you know all zoning restrictions and what you can and cannot do. Ascertain the exact wording and meaning of easements and other covenants which affect your property. Sometimes, if it's important, they can be changed or modified. However, that usually involves lawyers and considerable time and expense.

Resale value. Since the lot hasn't yet been bought or the house built, the idea of the resale value may be far from your mind. Still, unless you are absolutely certain that you'll want to spend the rest of your life in the place, the subject should at least be thought about. Granted, real estate values have been steadily rising for years and the trend is not likely to be reversed in the foreseeable future. But much of this increase in value is offset by the constantly rising inflation. If the time should come when, for one reason or another, you would want to or have to sell, is it the kind of place for which a buyer can readily be found?

Chapter 4
Strengths And Weaknesses Of Adobe

Remember when on visits to the sea as a child you built sand castles with all manner of turrets and carefully sculptured balconies, only to see all of your magnificent handiwork collapse upon itself with the first wave of the incoming tide?

Well, the same thing can happen to your adobe home unless you study and learn to understand the peculiarities of this unique building material, its strengths and its weaknesses.

ITS USES

Since time immemorial adobe has been used in a wide variety of different ways, but basically the methods of use can be divided into three classifications. One such method, probably the oldest and least satisfactory, is to simply mix the soil with sufficient water to produce a sticky paste and then to pour and shape that paste into long, narrow mounds. You let them dry and then repeat the process until something resembling a wall rises from the ground. This may have been a workable process when building a primitive igloo-type of shelter, but it is totally unsatisfactory for the kind of construction we think of today for even the simplest dwelling.

Another method known to have been used by the Indians and others is to prepare some sort of form from wood, branches or animal hides. Then fill this form with adobe mud and let it harden. Afterwards, the cast-form is removed. This is basically the method used in pouring premixed cement in the construction of modern buildings. A variation on the same idea, also used by some of the

Indians in centuries past, is to weave basket-like containers and pour the adobe mud into them. Let them dry and harden in the sun and then pile these more or less ball-shaped building blocks upon one another, smearing adobe over the whole thing to hold them together.

ADOBE BRICKS

This last method is, of course, the precurser of today's preferred method, namely the use of precast adobe bricks of a given size. The generally accepted dimensions of these bricks are 14 × 10 × 4 inches. They are produced by pouring the adobe mud into a wooden frame, removing the frame and then letting them dry in the sun. There is no particular reason why these bricks should be of the dimension noted above, except that smaller sizes would require vastly greater numbers of bricks to construct a given size wall and larger ones would be simply too heavy to be easily moved. As it is , a 14 × 10 × 4-inch adobe brick weighs 30 pounds.

No one knows how this particular proportion of the adobe brick was arrived at. It simply was the accepted size and brickmakers continued to use it as a standard, not worrying about the reason why. Interestingly enough, during some excavations in Egypt, adobe bricks were unearthed showing the same 14 × 10 × 4-inch dimension. Scientifically tested for age, they proved to be over 5,000 years old.

The adobe brick is the basic ingredient of any adobe structure built today. It can be purchased commercially from various companies. Most of these companies are located in New Mexico around the Santa Fe area. The price for the number of bricks needed to construct a given-size wall is comparable to the cost of standard bricks needed for a similar amount of square-footage.

Alternately, you can make them yourself and they won't cost you a thing, except the price of some rather basic tools and a transition period during which your muscles have to get used to working harder than they are likely to be used to.

TAKING IT STEP-BY-STEP

Before doing anything else, spend much time talking to people, people who are either in the process of building, or those who have done so. Also read all available material on the subject and get your head thoroughly filled with anything related to adobe. Not everyone you talk to or who's work you read will agree with everyone else. Concentrate on the ones who seem to make the most sense to you

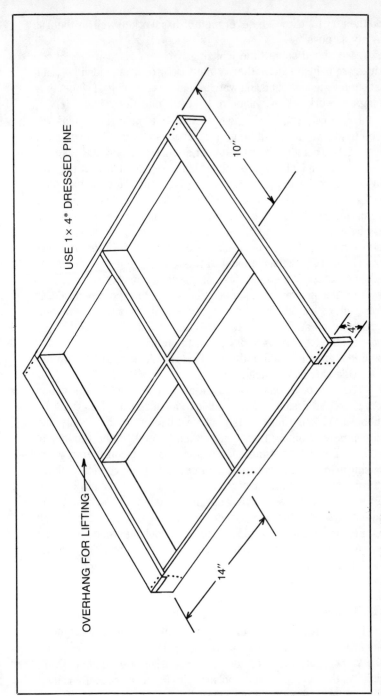

USE 1 × 4" DRESSED PINE

10"

4"

OVERHANG FOR LIFTING

14"

Fig. 4-1. Form for pouring adobe bricks.

71

and then try to follow whatever method has worked well for them as closely as possible.

Also spend some time kibitzing. Go to a place where abode bricks are being made, either commercially or by an individual, and just simply stand around and watch. Seeing is learning. If whoever is doing the work seems willing to talk, ask questions.

Eventually you'll be convinced that you know as much as you need to know, and you'll be getting anxious to get your own hands dirty. At this point get hold of someone with experience and take him to your chosen building site and let him get a good look at the soil. Not all the mud under your feet is necessarily ideal for making adobe bricks. Too much clay content will cause excessive shrinkage during the drying process, while too much sand may cause crumbling. It may be necessary to mix the soil available on your plot of land with some other soil from some nearby or even distant location. If you're not certain, mix a small amount of the selected soil with water and make just a few bricks, possibly using several different soil mixtures to arrive at a means of comparison. The more time you spend at this testing stage learning just how much water it takes to get the right consistency, learning to make a smooth mix and seeing how long it takes for the test bricks to dry under the temperature and humidity conditions at your location, the less likely it will be that you'll run into miscalculations and mistakes.

You have now come to a critical juncture in your transformation from an adobe dreamer and doodler to an adobe builder. Don't be stubborn. Making these tests may have been more hard work and more time consuming than you had anticipated. If the thought of multiplying this by the huge factor that must be considered when thinking in terms of an entire building seems beyond your capabilities in terms of either time or brute muscle power, you might be a lot better advised to dig into your savings account, pick up the phone and simply order the appropriate number of adobe bricks from a commercial supplier. You also better start looking around for some help, preferably people who have done this sort of work before and are either temporarily unemployed or want to earn some extra income.

BECOMING A BRICKMAKER

If, on the other hand, you are still willing to become a brickmaker before becoming a bricklayer, the next step is to make sure you've got whatever tools and materials are needed. Don't skimp on the quality. Lousy tools result in poor work and you'll be using them for months, if not years.

The Hardware

First you need something with which to level the piece of ground on your plot on which the adobe bricks will be poured and dried. A good rake will usually do the trick, although if the ground is quite uneven, you may need a shovel to remove protrusions, rocks or what have you.

You need a saw, a hammer, nails and some preferably dressed pine, to make the form into which the adobe is to be poured. A standard such form for homemade adobe bricks is usually designed to cast just four bricks at a time (Fig. 4-1). The reason is that it can be lifted off by one person. Any larger form would require two or more people.

A small hatchet or similar implement will come in handy later to trim irregularities from the nearly dry bricks.

Fig. 4-2. Adobe bricks piled up and drying at the Pecos National Monument. They will be used in the faithful restoration of the church ruin.

73

Get a heavy-duty wheelbarrow with a sufficiently large wheel to cause it to roll easily over uneven ground, even when fully loaded.

If running water is available at the site, fine. If not, you need a sufficiently large container to enable you to wash off the wooden form after each casting.

You'll need a hoe to work the mixture and possibly a pitchfork. So much for the hardware.

The Labor

Now you take your shovel and dig a pit. Whether it is round, square or any shape makes no difference. It should be about 2 or 3 feet deep and maybe 6 or 8 feet across. Into this pit goes your selected soil or mixture of soils. Water is poured on top of it in sufficient quantity to wet the whole mess. It is obvious by now that the availability of a nearby water supply of ample proportions is a virtual necessity. A lot of water is used in making adobe bricks and if all that water has to be carried for any appreciable distance, the chore could become too enormous to suffer.

The best advice is to let the soil soak in that water overnight. This is not absolutely necessary, but it is mandatory that all of the soil become thoroughly saturated. No dry clumps should ever find their way into the forms.

Once this saturation process is complete, a thin layer of straw may be sprinkled over the whole works. Then using the hoe, or bare feet if you happen to be a frustrated winemaker, the straw should be

Fig. 4-3. Air and wind continue the drying process of adobe bricks.

worked thoroughly into the wet mess. The use of straw in making adobe bricks has for some time been a matter of argument among the so-called experts. Some say it is unnecessary. Others insist on using it. The Indians traditionally used horse manure with its high content of very fine undigested straw fibers, but with horse manure rarely readily available these days, that idea should be shelved. Suitable substitutes for straw could be any number of tough-fibered grasses or other fibrous material. Generally speaking, it takes over one 100-pound bale of straw to make about 1,000 bricks.

If you've been reasonably thorough when making all those test bricks, you'll have found that the amount of water used to moisten the soil is fairly critical. It should be wet enough to be handled with the pitchfork. However, if it is too wet it will refuse to retain its shape when the form is removed, will buckle or "belly" at the edges and, in extreme cases, start to run.

You should now have a mixing pit full of adobe mud of the right consistency. You fill your wheelbarrow and pour it into the form which is lying on the smoothed-over piece of ground. A light layer of sand spread on the ground beforehand will help prevent the mud from sticking to the ground. The mixture should now be firmly

Fig. 4-4. Sun-dried adobe bricks are stacked and ready to use.

Fig. 4-5. Adobe bricks should be stacked where the ground is dry.

pressed into the form, making sure that it fills all corners. It is then smoothed across the top and any excess is removed.

It is usually a good idea, unless you have gone to the extra length of lining the form with tin, to have it thoroughly soaked in water before using it. This will help prevent the mud from sticking to the wood.

Okay. You're ready. Lift the form carefully and vertically off the ground. What remains are four adobe bricks. Wash the form with water and if you have a sufficient amount of level ground to work on, place it down again and cast another four.

The next step is transforming what is lying on the ground into usable bricks is up to the sun, weather and time. Even in dry climate with the sun shining every day, they will have to remain flat on the ground for several days until they are sufficiently dry and hard enough to be moved. If the weatherman predicts rain or if an anvil cloud in the far sky indicates the possibility of a thunderstorm with a sudden downpour, you may want to spread a plastic sheet over all of the bricks to keep them from getting any wetter than they are. But be sure to remove it as soon as the danger of rain has passed. Free air circulation is a must.

Fig. 4-6. It takes months for stacked adobe bricks to be thoroughly cured.

Once they have dried to the point that they can be picked up, they should be placed on edge, preferably with a little space between each one (Figs. 4-2 and 4-3). This will permit air and wind to continue the drying process. They will have to remain in this position for several more days, the longer the better. Like wine, they improve with age. In fact, it takes months for them to be thoroughly cured.

Two thoughts of precaution:

■ Stack the bricks somewhere where the ground is dry and where no water will collect in the event of rain (Figs. 4-4, 4-5 and 4-6).
■ Cover the top of the rows of stacked bricks with some waterproof material in a manner which will prevent water from running down the sides of the bricks, but don't envelop them so completely that the drying process will be inhibited.

So you're now an expert brickmaker. The next step comes in Chapter 5 and as we will explain, it is probably the most important in the whole process of building yourself a lasting and comfortable home.

Chapter 5

From The Bottom Up

In the same way in which water helps to make adobe, it also will eventually destroy it. In other words, the adobe brick which you will be using to build your house will have to be protected from contact with moisture to the greatest degree possible. Obviously, the greatest danger of moisture contamination is at ground level where the soil tends to be soaked every time it rains. It remains wet there for extended periods of time and water may collect in actual puddles, especially on the side of the house least exposed to the rays of the sun. In other words, your adobe house will have to be elevated above ground level. To accomplish this you need a foundation of material which is impervious to moisture.

THE FOUNDATION

Foundations serve a dual purpose. One, as already mentioned, is to keep the adobe away from the ground. The other is to support the not inconsiderable weight of the entire house. In order to accomplish the first, all that is needed is to build a foundation high enough to keep the bottom of the lowest adobe brick at least 10 to 15 inches above the surrounding surface. Accomplishing the second purpose is somewhat more difficult and before we go into some of the more complicated details, it might be well to suggest that consideration be given to having the foundation constructed by a professional. It may cost a bit more than doing the work yourself, but at least you can be reasonably certain that the whole thing isn't going to one day collapse around your ears.

Table 5-1. Number of Adobe Bricks Needed for Walls of Varying Thicknesses.

10-inch thick wall	257 bricks
14-inch thick wall	360 bricks
20-inch thick wall	514 bricks
24-inch thick wall	617 bricks
28-inch thick wall	720 bricks

Two types of materials are suitable for foundations, rock and concrete. Rock foundations—masses of reasonably flat rock piled one atop the other and secured with cement mortar—are esthetically more pleasing but unless extremely well constructed, could prove to be somewhat less durable. Concrete is less attractive but the more trouble-free of the two. For this reason, it is also by far the most popular in modern construction.

DIGGING THE TRENCH

Regardless of the material chosen, the first question which must be answered is: How deep down must a foundation go? If the ground is undisturbed, meaning that there is no fill anywhere in the area covered by the foundation, it must reach down far enough to be safely below the freezing level of the worst winter cold that can reasonably be expected in your area (Fig. 5-1). The reason is simple. When water freezes it expands, and if the moisture under the foundation should suddenly freeze, it might succeed in raising the foundation. A shift of as little as ⅛ inch can result in unpleasant cracks in the plaster all over the house. Any local contractor should be able to give you a fair estimate of the depth to which the foundation trench must be dug.

The digging of the trench itself is best done by a trench-digging machine. You can hire a man who owns one to do the job for you, or you can probably rent one from one of the local equipment rental places. Be sure to let the man show you how to use it because they are a bit complicated.

The trench itself should be about 8 inches wider than the planned thickness of the wall. It must be dug everywhere where a load-bearing wall is to be erected. Special consideration should be given for fireplaces and such, but more about that later. If there are soft spots or any areas of fill in the way of the foundation line, they must be excavated down to the level of undisturbed earth. Or later they must be bridged by a separate concrete beam of greater strength than the concrete used for the basic foundation. This beam will have to extend far enough to be supported on both ends by undisturbed soil.

THE WALLS

How thick should you build a wall? In trying to answer this question, a number of considerations should be kept in mind. The most basic has to do with the bearing strength which is required. Most of the weight of the entire structure must be supported by the outside walls. Experts seem to differ on what they consider an adequate thickness, but using the bricks lengthwise, which results in a 10-inch wall, is thought by some to be insufficient for outside walls. By turning them the other way we end up with a 14-inch wall which is adequate for a single-story structure.

THE SECOND STORY

If a second story is planned, or even just thought about as a possible future addition, walls of greater thickness may be indicated. Depending on how the bricks are layed, walls of 10, 14, 20 (Fig. 5-2), 24 (Fig. 5-3) or 28 inches (Fig. 5-4) can easily be built. The only prerequisite is a foundation of the appropriate thickness to carry the wall and, of course, the availability of the required number of bricks.

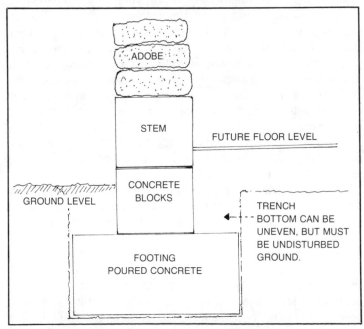

Fig. 5-1. Digging and pouring a foundation for your adobe home.

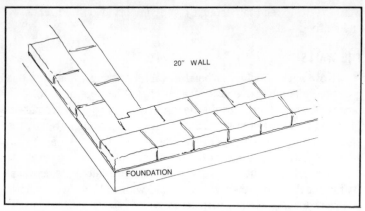

Fig. 5-2. A 20-inch thick foundation wall.

To figure out the number of bricks needed, divide the horizontal measure of the wall(s) by the width (length) of the bricks and then multiply by the number of 4-inch layers needed to reach the required height.

Table 5-1 offers a general guide to the number of adobe bricks needed for a 10 × 10-foot section of wall of varying thicknesses. Don't worry about windows and doors. There is always a certain amount of breakage and waste from cutting.

Aside from the purely practical considerations of the bearing strength of the walls, a greater wall thickness has two other advantages. One is the exceptional insulating quality of adobe. In areas with considerable temperature extremes during hot summers and cold winters, the extra cost of a thick wall will eventually pay dividends in terms of greater indoor comfort and lower heating or air conditioning bills.

The other consideration is purely esthetic. Thick walls are quite beautiful and much of the unique charm of traditional old adobes is the result of their massiveness (Fig. 5-5).

When the trench is ready it is time to start pouring concrete. Concrete is a mixture of cement, sand, gravel and water and different proportions will result in differing bearing strengths. Again, unless you really know what you are doing, don't be proud—let an expert advise you as to the strength needed and let an expert do the pouring. If your plot is adequately accessible, you can contract with one of those people who operate ready-mix trucks. They will drive the truck right up to the site and pour the concrete through a chute which is part of the equipment included with the truck. If for some reason that is not possible, the concrete will have to be off-loaded into wheelbarrows and transported by hand. This is not an easy job, to put it mildly, especially if it involves an uphill grade.

Steel reinforcing bars, called *rebars*, must be embedded into the concrete and stick out far enough to subsequently hold the cement blocks in place. The concrete portion of the foundation simply consti-

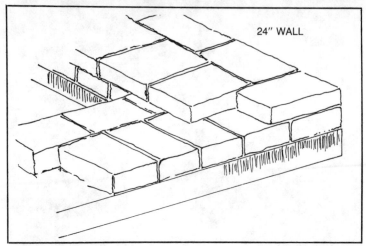

Fig. 5-3. A 24-inch thick foundation wall.

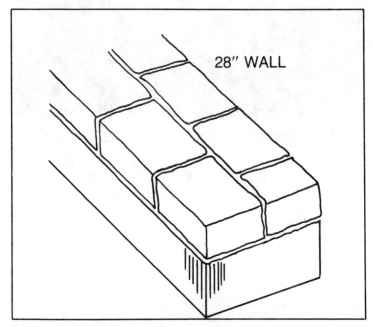

Fig. 5-4. A 28-inch thick foundation wall.

Fig. 5-5. The extra thickness of the double-brick wall is clearly visible in this view through a window of the north patio.

tutes the footing. This is the base on which the whole structure is going to rest. Once it is in place you're still not ready to proceed with those beautiful adobe bricks which have been patiently hardening somewhere nearby.

The next step involves what is referred to as the stem. It is the very bottom portion of your actual wall. It usually consists of two rows of concrete blocks, one atop the other. When in place they are filled with concrete. They are held in place by the rebars inside and become an integral part of the foundation. The top of the upper row of these concrete blocks should be 10 to 12 inches above the ground. This represents the base for the actual adobe wall. Since this is likely to be somewhat above the level of the eventual interior floors, you may want to remember to omit the upper cement blocks in places where doors are planned, or you may subsequently have to chip them down to the level of the floor.

An alternate means of constructing a foundation is to pour a solid concrete slab under the entire house, or at least part of it, such as the area which will eventually be the garage. Before such a slab can be poured, the ground must be prepared by clearing it of grass and all manner of vegetation which might gradually decay or permit the slab to settle and possibly crack. A wooden form must be built to the height to which the concrete is to be poured. The upper edges must be level because they will serve as a means of smoothing the concrete and removing excess.

Again, this is really a job for an expert. Most amateur builders would be best advised to pay to have it done by someone who knows what he is doing. Skilled concrete contractors are not that expensive. Remember, you'll have to live with the final result for a very long time.

Chapter 6
Building Your Adobe Home

Now we finally get to the part we've been preparing for all this time. We're going to build a house. What is really meant by this is that we're ready to start piling all of those adobe bricks one on top of the other. But this too, isn't quite as simple as it sounds. First we need mortar to glue the bricks to one another.

To make mortar we use the same soil mixture that was used to prepare the bricks. Bits of rock and extraneous matter were of no particular importance in making the bricks, but it must be removed from the mortar mix. To do this the mix should be strained through a sufficiently fine screen to eliminate any such matter exceeding a ¼ inch in size. Once that has been accomplished the mortar is spread in a thickness of approximately ½ to ¾ of an inch atop the foundation stem and the first row of adobe bricks is layed on top. Then comes another layer of mortar and the second row can be started.

WALLS

Be sure to offset the bricks in such a way that the vertical cracks between bricks are at least 4 or more inches away from one another (Fig. 6-1). Do not fill these vertical spaces with mortar. Later on, when you apply the outer coating of adobe or some other kind of plaster, it will seep into these vertical spaces and thus adhere to the wall without the need for wire mesh.

While it is relatively simple to lay the first few rows of bricks in a straight line, the higher the wall gets, the easier it becomes to cause a slight lean in one direction or another. Unless corrected early, the immense weight of the wall will eventually cause it to collapse. To avoid this, drive wooden stakes vertically into the ground at both ends of the wall. Use a plumb line to make sure that they are truly vertical. Then tie a string between the two stakes at the level at which you happen to be working. Lay the bricks along that string.

Don't lay more than five or six rows of bricks on top of one another at any one point on any one day (Fig. 6-2). If you do, the still-wet mortar may be squeezed together before it has a chance to harden and your wall may end up being a mess of unsightly wavy lines. In addition, such compression of the mortar and the resulting unevenness will be detrimental to the bearing strength of the wall.

As long as the top of the wall on which you are working is no more than about waist high, the work is relatively easy. This is assuming that you consider lifting hundreds of 30-pound blocks easy. However, once it gets higher than that, the task should really be handled by two people. One should prepare and spread the mortar, the other should climb up and down ladders with the bricks.

WINDOWS AND DOORS

But a house, in order to be livable, must not have only walls. There are doors and windows to be considered, places where one

Fig. 6-2. Do not lay more than five or six courses of bricks at a time. The mortar in the lower courses has to dry somewhat before it can support the weight of additional bricks.

88

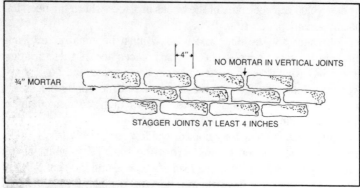

Fig. 6-1. Bricks must be offset by 4 or more inches.

may eventually wish to secure cabinets to the wall and so on. Contrary to many other building materials, you can't nail anything to an adobe wall. For this reason, anything that is to be attached to the wall must be thought of and planned for in advance.

The material best suited for this purpose is wood. It is therefore logical that in the appropriate places, wood sections must be incorporated into the wall. These can be flat 1-inch thick pieces inserted horizontally between the layers of bricks. Or they can be so-called *gringo blocks*, pieces of wood of the same thickness as the adobe

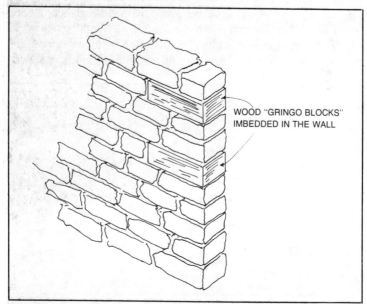

Fig. 6-3. Gringo blocks are often embedded in the walls of an adobe house.

bricks which replace some of the bricks in places where the need for nailing is anticipated (Fig. 6-3).

A frame for the door and window must be constructed from lumber. Be sure to nail some diagonal pieces across these frames (Fig. 6-4) to assure that they remain rectangular and don't start leaning in one direction or the other. Build the adobe blocks up against the frame four or five courses (rows) high and then continue the wall building away from the opening.

Any such opening for a door or window requires *lintels*. Lintels are horizontal wooden beams across the top. These must be of sufficient strength to carry the load of the wall and the roof portion that will be built up above them (Figs. 6-5 through 6-9).

Back to the lintels. Usually 6 × 8-inch planks are used. Two of them stand on edge side by side, with at least l foot on each end resting on the wall itself. They may either be placed in a manner which will keep them exposed after the structure is finished (Fig. 6-10) or their combined width may be as much as 4 inches narrower than the wall. This would permit you to subsequently cover them with narrow strips of adobe brick.

Traditionally, windows in the old adobes were small. They were simply tiny ventilation holes with no covering except possibly some animal hides in the winter. Then when first mica and later glass became available, the Indians built somewhat larger windows into their adobes. But even those windows, by modern standards, are rather limited in size and number.

Today most of us like a lot of light. But the summer sun can get uncomfortably hot in most areas in which adobe building is prevalent

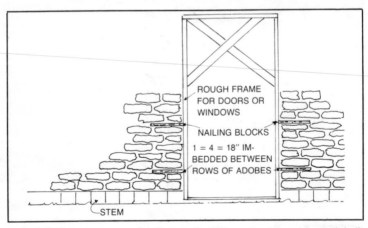

ROUGH FRAME
FOR DOORS OR
WINDOWS

NAILING BLOCKS
1 = 4 = 18" IM-
BEDDED BETWEEN
ROWS OF ADOBES

STEM

Fig. 6-4. Door and window frames must be built of wood and the adobe walls built around them.

Fig. 6-6. A solid wooden beam is used as the lintel.

Fig. 6-7. Lintels are shimmed on one side with left-over pieces of plywood in order to attain a perfect level.

Fig. 6-5. An opening is left for the future window in this adobe home currently under construction.

and the cold winters of the high-altitude desert and mountain regions bring their cold into the house through the windows. The windows also offer considerably less insulative effect than the thick adobe walls.

It doesn't much matter at this stage of building whether you will eventually opt for single- or double-pane windows because either will fit into the frames set into the wall. But if you like a lot of light and want large and numerous window openings, the extra cost of double-pane windows may pay meaningful dividends in the long run.

Fig. 6-8. Nailing blocks have been incorporated into the wall to hold the future window frame.

Fig. 6-9. A completed window opening awaits its window frame.

Fig. 6-10. In this photograph of a window opening in an adobe wall, the lintels are left exposed. Note the pieces of screening nailed over spots where non-adobe material, such as wood shims, would cause the adobe-mud plaster to fail to adhere to the wall surface.

They are a bit harder to keep clean, but then, nothing is perfect.

Once all bearing walls have been built up to the height of the future indoor ceiling, provisions must be made to support the vigas. The vigas support the ceiling material on which the roof will eventually be built. Adobe has only minimal resistance to compression and therefore the vigas cannot simply be placed on top of the highest course of adobe bricks. What is needed is a continuous support which will distribute the weight of the vigas, ceiling and roof evenly across the entire length of the walls. This can be accomplished by either pouring a concrete beam (Fig. 6-11) or by placing a heavy wooden beam along the top of all bearing walls.

In order to pour a concrete beam (Fig. 6-12), a wooden form has to be constructed and held in place by some sort of brackets (usually metal). The concrete is then poured into the form. A rebar should be incorporated into the concrete for extra strength. Once the concrete has sufficiently cured, vigas can be laid atop it, and adobe bricks built up on top of it around the vigas to a height of about twelve or more inches above the top of the vigas (Figs. 6-13 and 6-14).

94

Most adobe structures have flat roofs. This means that the ceiling and roof are built up directly on top of the vigas, with no open space in between (Fig. 6-15). It goes without saying that such roofs must have a sufficient grade in one direction or the other. This will cause water and melting snow to run off and not stand on the roof in puddles which would eventually cause even the best constructed roof to begin to leak. It does not have to be much of a grade. A few inches will do.

In many instances this grade is achieved as a logical result of the fact that vigas, being actually tree trunks, are thinner on one side than on the other. By laying then all with the thin side in the same direction, a certain amount of slope will be created at the top while the bottom remains level. If this degree of slope should appear to be insufficient, or if finished round, square or rectangular beams are to be used, the slope will have to be provided for in the supporting concrete beam. The form into which the concrete is to be poured must also allow for it.

While more attractive wooden beams can be used in place of the concrete, they may be less satisfactory. All wood continues to shrink for very long periods of continuous gradual drying. This could possibly result in some cracks long after the house is finished. Also, unless beams of sufficient length can be found to go from one end of

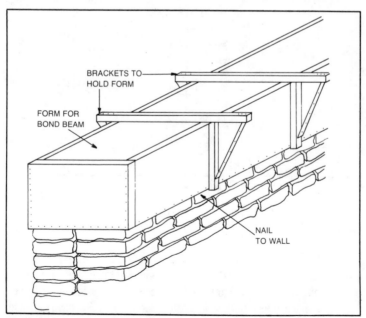

Fig. 6-12. Form for a concrete bond beam.

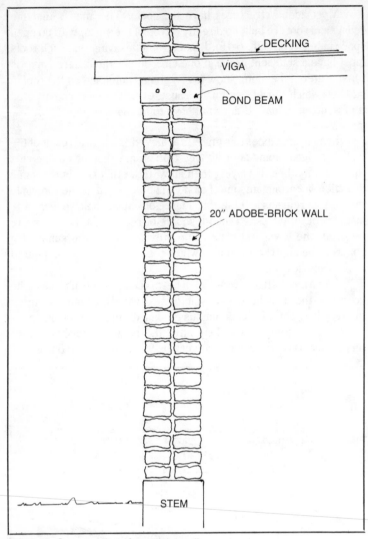

Fig. 6-13. Cross section of an adobe wall.

the wall to the other, they must be carefully spliced to turn pieces into several continuous beams which won't have a tendency to sag at the joint.

So far we have talked only about bearing walls—the walls which must carry the weight of the entire building. There are, of course, other walls in a home. There are walls which are designed to act strictly as partitions between individual rooms. Originally all of these walls were also constructed of adobe, usually of a somewhat thinner

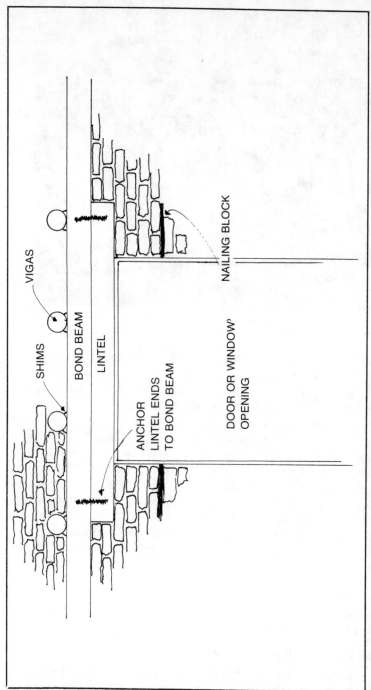

SHIMS

VIGAS

BOND BEAM

LINTEL

ANCHOR
LINTEL ENDS
TO BOND BEAM

NAILING BLOCK

DOOR OR WINDOW
OPENING

Fig. 6-14. Bricks are built up atop the bond beam to form the parapet.

Fig. 6-11. Although adobe brick is used in the construction of this home, concrete blocks are used for the top of the walls.

width than the outside walls. Using adobe throughout the house gives a pleasant effect of unity of construction. It also results in effective sound proofing, a characteristic which may be especially desirable if certain parts of the home will be children's quarters where an inevitable racket can be expected.

On the other hand, expediency may demand a simpler type of construction for these walls. Curtain walls, which are wooden frames covered with plaster board or some other such material, can be easily constructed lying flat on the ground. They are then raised into their appropriate position and subsequently bolted to the floor and ceiling. Such walls are easier and quicker to build, cost somewhat less and take up a little less floor space. With a large number of such partitions, this can add up to a considerable amount. They also simplify the installation of electrical wiring and the placement of electrical outlets and switches.

The choice is yours. If sound proofing and the unity of structural appearance are more important than time and money, by all means use adobe throughout the house.

ARE WALLS REALLY NECESSARY?

In a currently popular television series called "Vegas", the hero lives in what appears to be a converted warehouse. It consists of one

Fig. 6-15. The vigas are in place atop this immense future living room. The large picture window in the back wall has necessitated angling the bond beam over its top. It is the same case with the large fireplace which is constructed of concrete blocks and set into the wall at the right.

huge room, divided by plants and groups of furniture, where he works, lives, sleeps and keeps his car. It is also where his assistant spends her days answering the phone. There isn't a wall in this whole combination living, working, sleeping and garage area, yet it all looks rather charming.

Some younger couples building adobe homes in outlying areas seem to find a similar arrangement attractive and livable. They'll simply build the outside walls around a large space which is divided by furnishings and possibly different floor levels for sleeping, living, cooking and eating areas. There are no interior walls except possibly one to shut off the bathroom.

Frequently the owners of such homes will find that sooner or later they will want to add other rooms to this one-room complex, especially if children are born. They will require a place in which to take their naps and sleep at night while the rest of the family is still up and about.

The initial advantage is that such a one-room enclosure can be built rather cheaply and in comparatively little time. It can then be lived in while the rest of the house begins to grow as the need arises. The disadvantage is that there is no privacy. Certainly not everyone can stand being around other people, even loved ones, all day and all night.

Chapter 7
Under Foot

Every home has to have some sort of floor finish and the character of adobe construction lends itself to a wide variety of such finishes (Fig. 7-1).

FLOORS

Traditionally the Indians didn't bother to build floors at all. They simply leveled and smoothed the floors by tamping the earth down with moccasined or bare feet. They wet it repeatedly with water or animal blood (for color) or a mixture of the two until it became a solid surface of adobe.

In such houses one would step across a threshold and down into the room, rather than continuing on a level with the base of the door opening. While this method is by far the cheapest and easiest, it is no longer considered adequate in the context of modern living.

BRICK FLOORING

In the modern adobe one of the most attractive types of floor covering is brick. Although not exactly cheap, it is easy to lay and if treated correctly, easy to maintain.

In order to produce a satisfactory brick floor, the surface beneath needs some preparation. First you should gather all of the left-over dirt from the excavation of the foundation channel and pile it inside. Usually that will be sufficient to raise the surface to a level which, when the bricks are added, will bring the floor level with the base of the door openings.

Fig. 7-1. Adobe construction lends itself to a wide variety of floor finishes.

The desired level of the subfloor is some 3½ inches below the level of the final floor. It should be scribed on the inside of the foundation stem. Then the dirt should be wetted repeatedly, raked to an even surface and stamped down in order to eventually have it compact into a reasonably smooth, level and hard surface. It will probably require repeated shaving of protrusions and filling of spaces which have sunk below the desired level. It is important that this be done with patience and care since the weight of the bricks and that of the people walking on them will cause them to settle unevenly if the subsurface is not hard enough and insufficiently smooth.

All soil, no matter how hardened, is full of all kinds of bugs and other potentially living matter. To prevent these beasts from deciding at one point to start crawling up through the cracks between the bricks, the entire surface should now be sprinkled rather liberally with some kind of insecticide, such as chlordane (Fig. 7-2). Don't be chintzy with that stuff. Be sure that there is at least some of it everywhere.

The next step is to spread a plastic sheet over the entire area. This will act as a vapor barrier. Such material is available in rolls of widths sufficient for even the largest room area, even up to 40 or more feet. Ask for four-mil thickness when buying it. The width to select when buying the roll should be the width, not length, of your largest room. Preferably it should be a few inches wider. The edges need not be cut to the exact dimensions, but may be lapped a few inches.

The next material you need is dry sand. Spread dry sand to a thickness of about 1 to 1½ inches over the entire surface. Damp sand is no good because it tends to fail to fill small depressions and can therefore eventually result in an uneven floor. This sand should be leveled quite carefully. One method to use would be to lay two pipes from one end of the room to the other and then slide a 2 × 4 or other screed across them. Later, when the pipes have been removed, the narrow channels left can be filled by pouring sand into them.

FLOOR PATTERN

Now we are ready for the bricks. The bricks to use are referred to as *solids* or *patio type*. Regular common building brick is full of holes which help to hold mortar. This would not be desirable as a floor because it would become a receptacle for all manner of dirt. Before putting down the first brick, you may want to think about the pattern to be used (Fig. 7-3). Most bricks are not exactly twice as long as they are wide, therefore it might be a good idea to use any old

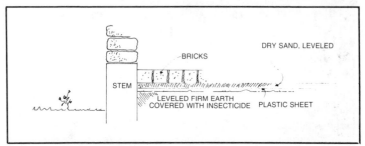

Fig. 7-2. This cross section of a brick floor illustrates the leveled firm earth covered with insecticide.

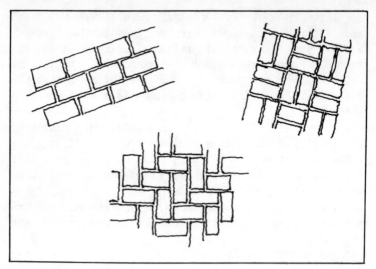

Fig. 7-3. Various patterns for brick floors.

flat surface outside and put down a few bricks in a variety of patterns. See how it works and how you like the looks of the results.

Then, once you have decided on a pattern, start in the center of a door opening and work forward and outward. Most likely, when getting to the wall, you will find that you need to cut some bricks in order to fill spaces into which they won't fit. There are brick chisels and either dry or wet masonry saws to do this job, but it requires patience and care.

Handling bricks eventually becomes murder on the hands. Some kind of covering may be needed unless you've got the skin of an elephant. Some people like to work with gloves. Another method I have heard about is to tape the inside of the fingers with surgical tape. Unless you are a confirmed masochist, you're sure to figure out a means of protection that suits you best.

It is a good idea to plan your time so that you can finish one room in a day and not let it sit there half done throughout a night or two. Once it's done, keep walking on the new floor to a minimum, because it is necessary to sweep fine sand into the cracks between the bricks. This firmly locks them into one another, especially in the areas which will eventually receive the maximum amount of traffic. If that is not done the bricks will tend to shift slightly, resulting in uneven spaces between them and an unsightly overall appearance.

Now the floor is technically ready to be used, although most home owners prefer to add a sealer. Without sealing, the brick floor retains a dull appearance and is exceedingly difficult to keep clean. It may *be* clean, but it won't *look* clean. When mentioning sealers you are likely to get all kinds of contradicting advice as to the ideal product and method to be used. Try anything that appeals to you, but there is a product called Floor Hardener by the Standard Oil Company which can be applied with a paint roller. Bricks are porous and you'll be using considerable quantities of this hardener. A gallon will barely be sufficient for a first coat in a 12 by 15-foot room. It will take two coats at least to effect good sealing of the floor, but you can repeat the process as often as you like. Each additional coat will darken the color of the floor by a small degree (Fig. 7-4).

Subsequently the floor can be kept shiny and clean with standard wax or liquid plastic available in any supermarket. Wax eventually builds up into unsightly yellowish white spots or streaks. Clear liquid plastic products seem to avoid or, at least, lessen that problem.

CONCRETE FLOOR

If you don't like brick, there are a number of alternate choices. The simplest, of course, is a solid concrete slab. It can be poured directly on the undisturbed ground below. It should be of approximately a 4-inch thickness except at places where it has to carry heavy loads, such as the location of a future fireplace. Twelve inches or more may be needed there.

Fig. 7-4. A brick floor in a semicircular den, referred to as the kiva room. Note the fireplace in the far wall, the bench-type seating arrangement built into the wall and the double-brick thickness of the wall itself.

Concrete floors aren't exactly a thing of beauty and no matter how much care was taken in the preparation and pouring, they will eventually crack in a few places. A raw concrete floor is fine in a garage or carport, but it is really unacceptable in living spaces. If most of the area is to be covered by one or a collection of carpets or rugs, there should be sponge-rubber or other padding under the rugs to reduce that feeling of hardness that comes with concrete. Not only is that unpleasant, it is eventually tiring to walk on.

On the other hand, a concrete slab can serve as a base for all sorts of alternate floor coverings. It can be used under a brick floor, although this would seem unwarranted unless the slab is already in place. If that is the case, the portion of the floor to be covered with brick may end up being a shallow step higher than the rest of the floor. Flagstone can be used to create a good effect in areas which border on sliding doors leading to a patio or other outdoor areas. I suppose one could lay wood across a concrete slab, but that, too, seems to be a rather silly way of constructing a wood floor.

CERAMIC TILE

One type of covering that is particularly decorative and lends itself well to the overall style of adobe is ceramic tile (Fig. 7-5). It can be beautiful and it is durable. Its major drawback is its expense. Ready-made tile in all conceivable designs and colors is available from many sources in the United States or it can be imported from Mexico.

When using tile the subfloor is of particular importance because any unevenness or softness will result in a buckling of the floor and possible cracking of some of the tiles. A concrete slab is by far the most desirable type of underfloor, although a well prepared and thoroughly hardened mud floor can be used. Whatever is used as a base, its top should be just a sufficient distance below the base of the door openings. This should allow for the thickness of the tile and the mortar-material used to attach the tile to the surface beneath. This mortar, usually a damp four-to-one mixture of sand and portland cement, is spread over the base. Cover a reasonably small area at a time. It dries rather slowly, giving you time to level the top surface to an even smoothness and then to set the tiles, one at a time. The tiles must be tapped firmly into place with some sort of resilient instrument, preferably a rubber hammer. Some mortar should be put into the joints between the tiles and the excess should be carefully wiped away with a damp rag to avoid stains which will be difficult to remove later on. For several days after laying the tiles the joints should be dampened over and over again in order to prevent

Fig. 7-5. Ceramic tile makes an elegant floor in a bathroom.

the mortar from drying too fast. If it dried too quickly, it would weaken the bond between it and the base.

While it would probably be excessive to plan on doing all floors in a house with ceramic tile, they do lend a rich decorative touch to areas around fireplaces, in bathrooms, entrance halls or other spaces of moderate dimensions.

VINYL MATERIALS

Other types of covering, often preferred in kitchens, bathrooms and possibly children's playrooms, are the various vinyl materials. They are available in a wide variety of colors and patterns, either in the form of individual vinyl tiles or in continuous rolls of adequate width. Some vinyl tiles even come with self-adhesive backing. This makes application easy as well as reduces messiness to an absolute minimum. While laying individual tiles on a smooth and carefully cleaned base is an easy matter that can be accomplished by any amateur with a minimum of problems, laying down entire sheets is an extremely ticklish operation and should really be left to a professional. In either case, the importance of the smoothness of the base cannot be emphasized too strongly. These materials are thin and quite flexible and any indentation or protrusion, no matter how slight, will eventually be reproduced in the surface of the covering.

WOOD FLOORS

Wood floors tend to give the impression of being softer and warmer than any of the hard materials mentioned so far. But a good wood floor is an expensive undertaking and requires a considerable amount of preparation. Usually wood floors are found in houses with basements or at least crawl spaces beneath. They are rarely found in houses set directly on the undisturbed ground. To construct a wood floor, a subflooring must first be built with supports leading to the undisturbed ground below. This will support the actual floor and those who will eventually walk on it. This subfloor can be made of plywood of adequate thickness (5/8 to 3/4 inch) or 1-inch lumber laid diagonally across the joists. Subsequently the lumber to be used in the actual hardwood flooring is then nailed directly to the subfloor, preferably at 90- or 45-degree angles to the boards used in the subfloor. Of course, this would not apply if the subfloor is plywood. Most hardwood flooring can be purchased with tongue-in-groove sides. They provide a tight fit which is made even tighter by toenailing through the groove.

Much of the cost of such a floor depends on the quality of the wood selected. If eventual wall-to-wall carpeting is anticipated, the surface appearance of the wood is of no great consideration. If, on the other hand, large areas of the floor are going to be in plain sight, the texture and grain of the wood can add immeasurably to the beauty of the room. The extra expense for fine woods would be money well spent in that case.

Chapter 8
Over Head

Where there is a floor there is usually a ceiling and ceilings in adobe buildings can be works of true beauty (Figs. 8-1, 8-2 and 8-3). The most beautiful, in my opinion, are those which most closely resemble the ceiling construction used by the Indians in the early days of adobe building.

VIGAS

Once having built up their walls, they would hoist *vigas* — tree trunks from which all branches and bark had been stripped — to the top of the walls (Fig. 8-4). They would place them a given distance apart from one another and then cover them with *latillas*. Latillas are slim tree branches placed quite close together. Together, the vigas and latillas formed the base for the roof which was usually simply a several foot thick layer of adobe mud.

Today this same basic principle is still being used in modern adobe structures. A number of shortcuts have been introduced to simplify and speed up construction, although in many cases, this also reduces the visual beauty of the ceiling.

Vigas can be purchased from commercial suppliers in varying lengths and thicknesses. Depending on the distance from bearing wall to bearing wall which they must cover, they should be adequate thickness to support the weight of the roof itself. Vigas with an average diameter of 6 inches are considered sufficient for a 10-foot span. Longer spans require greater thicknesses: 8 inches for 15 or 16 feet; 10 inches for 20 feet; and so on.

Fig. 8-1. A ceiling in an adobe home is often a work of great beauty.

Moving the vigas from the ground to the top of the wall can be a bit of a chore because of their not inconsiderable weight. Self-propelled lifting machinery that are used in warehouses and in the loading of trucks are called *forklifts*. Some of them are capable of raising their loads to a sufficient height. Forklifts can be rented, but be sure that they are capable of lifting the vigas to a height several inches above the top of the wall. Also, the ground around the building has to be sufficiently level to permit maneuvering the forklift.

If an adequate forklift is not available, or if the surrounding terrain does not permit using one, there are a number of other means of getting the vigas up there. One possibility would be to erect wooden hoists. These are wood beams vertically set into the ground and firmly supported by guy wires. Across the top of these beams another beam is placed horizontally and firmly secured. Two winches are attached to it. Then, using heavy rope, the vigas can then be winched up to the required level.

If that seems too complicated, there is another and simpler way, but this one must be handled with a bit of extra caution since there are certain inherent dangers involved. Two vigas or other strong, smooth beams are layed at an angle against the side of the wall (Fig. 8-5). The longer the viga or beam used for this, the shallower the angle at which it rests against the wall and the easier the work. The next step is to firmly anchor two ropes at the top of the wall.

Fig. 8-2. The ceiling in this adobe home helps to accent the chandelier.

Fig. 8-3. Unique ceilings are frequently found in adobe homes.

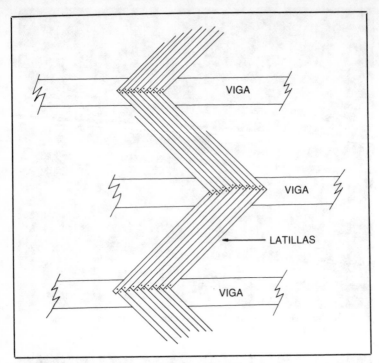

Fig. 8-4. Details of a ceiling as seen from the top.

The first of the vigas to be raised is then placed at the bottom of the two beams, at right angles to them. The rope is dropped down from the top of the wall where one end is anchored. It is fed underneath the viga to be raised. The loose end is then thrown back up to the men atop the wall. The two workers stationed on top of the wall then pull the loose ends of the two ropes, making sure that each pulls at the same speed. The viga will gradually roll up the angled beams.

The dangers mentioned are these:

■ Don't stand too close to where the viga will eventually drop off the top of the angled beam and onto the top of the wall. If you do, you are in danger of having it drop on your foot. Needless to say, that could be less than pleasant.

■ Don't sit on top of the wall or you may end up with a lap full of viga.

■ Persons below, helping to push and guide the viga up the incline, should be aware that there is always the possibility of a rope breaking, an anchor coming loose or one of the men at the top suddenly having to sneeze or losing his footing.

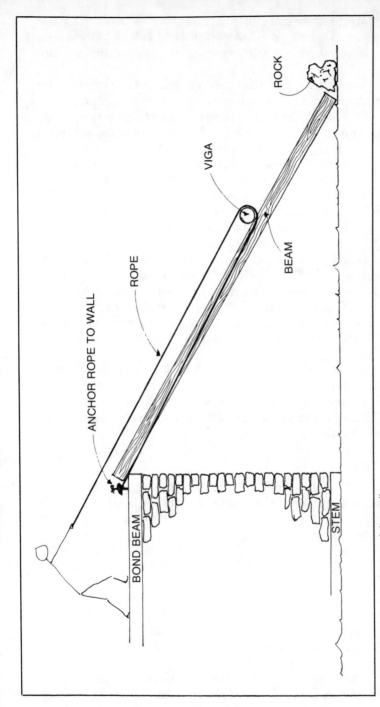

Fig. 8-5. Lifting vigas to the top of the walls.

Whatever the cause, there is always the possibility that the viga could come tumbling down. Anyone unlucky enough to stand in its way is likely to remember that experience for longer than he will care to.

Remember that all vigas have a thicker and a thinner end. Be sure that they are placed with all the thin ends in the same direction. They should be in the direction in which the roof is supposed to slope in order to permit water to run off. Once they are up there, it would be virtually impossible to turn them around.

If all that will eventually go on top of the vigas is the roof, it is generally considered adequate to space them 3 to 4 feet apart. On the other hand, if a second story is planned, they should be placed at 2 to 3-foot intervals to potentially form a firm base for the upper floor (Fig. 8-6). This should be done even if the second story is only a vague idea for some distant future addition.

In order to achieve the traditional adobe look, the vigas should stick out a foot or more beyond the outside wall, especially on the thin side. The thin side is where the vigas will eventually support the *canales*. The canales are the drains that permit the water to run off of the roof. If these canales and their supporting viga ends are too short, the wind may blow the run-off water against the side of the house, thus playing havoc with the adobe wall.

Once placed at the appropriate intervals, they can be secured in place with small shims to prevent them from rolling short distances in one direction or the other. The next step is to build up the adobe wall around the vigas to a level of three or more courses above the top of the vigas.

CEILINGS

You now have the base for a beautiful ceiling. What happens next will determine its true beauty for all the years you intend to live in the house. The choice which must be made is a matter of what type of decking to put on top of the vigas. The simplest might seem to be long boards, layed at right angles to the vigas, from one end of the room to the other. Tongue-in-groove flooring-type lumber can be used for this purpose, but employing this method may seem simpler than it actually is. The problem which develops immediately is the fact that virtually all vigas are not ruler-straight. Some will stick up an inch or more while others may have a slight bend downward. This will make the job of nailing long, straight boards to their tops rather difficult.

An alternative is to use short lengths of board. Cut them at a 45-degree angle at each end and place them at 45-degree angles atop

Fig. 8-6. If a second story is planned, the appropriate spacing of vigas takes on added importance.

the vigas. This creates a kind of herringbone effect. It is not only more attractive to look at, but also eliminates most of the problems caused by the unevenness of the vigas. The fact that the resulting ceiling is not perfectly level is of no importance because it will be virtually impossible to see that from below.

To my mind the most beautiful ceiling can be constructed by using a slightly improved version of the old Indian method. In other words, use latillas. You may be able to purchase reasonably straight, thin branches from about 1 inch to 1½ inches in diameter that are already cleaned of bark, branches and other protrusions. Or you may have to get a permit and go out into the woods and cut them yourself. It takes many individual pieces laid at a 45-degree angle across the vigas to achieve what will appear as a solid ceiling. Whether purchased commercially or gathered and prepared by yourself, they should be thoroughly treated with some sort of effective insecticide to kill and eliminate whatever living organisms may exist in the various cracks.

Today few builders bother with this method, but exceptionally beautiful examples of it can be found in old adobes, especially in some of the old Indian-Spanish churches.

Fig. 8-7. Ceiling detail from a home, still under construction, in which the builder is making greater than average use of concrete blocks in addition to adobe. Here the bond beam has been cast, topped by concrete blocks into which the roof beams have been embedded. High quality tongue-in-groove finished lumber has been used for the decking.

Many builders today prefer finished rectangular beams to the raw round vigas. To lift them to roof height requires either a hoist or a forklift. Obviously. They cannot be rolled up some angled incline. Aside from that, they are used in the same way as vigas and require approximately the same dimensions and distance from one another. The big advantage is that they are perfectly straight and smooth. They can be decked with long boards with no difficulty. In conjunction with such beams, long boards placed at right angles to them produce a perfectly satisfactory effect.

Whether the ceiling atop the vigas or beams consists of standard board lumber, or of latillas, it requires considerable build-up on top to produce a lasting and weather-proof roof (Fig. 8-7). There will be more about this shortly.

INTERIOR FINISH FOR YOUR CEILINGS

The eventual interior finish of such a viga or beam ceiling is a matter of individual taste. In most cases they are simply stained with

Fig. 8-8. Viga ceilings simplify the hanging of planters or other decorative items.

some sort of varnish that brings out the color and texture of the wood itself. Some people like to paint the spaces between the vigas or beams, while others have been known to paint everything. Only remember, once painted, it is an incredibly difficult, time-consuming, frustrating and expensive job to strip the paint away.

I have seen some older adobe homes in which owners or former owners for some incomprehensible reason decided to cover a perfectly good viga ceiling with flat ceiling boards. This makes it look on the inside like any old house. Personally I think that is sacrilege, but then there is no accounting for individual tastes.

One of the marvelous advantages of a viga or beam ceiling is the ability to hang things from it, such as planters or chandeliers (Fig. 8-8). Hooks can be screwed into the beams or vigas with ease. Even if they are removed at some later date, the holes are likely to not show at all. If they do, they can easily be filled with a dab of plastic wood. This same method can be used on the walls to hang heavy

Fig. 8-9. Few things are as important in building a home as a well-constructed roof.

pictures, cabinets and the like. This is an important advantage since nailing adequate supports for such free-hanging weights into an adobe wall may be difficult, if not impossible.

KEEPING DRY

Few things can make life quite as miserable as a leaking roof (Fig. 8-9). That sudden drip-drip in some obscure corner of a room, or just where you have placed your favorite chair, is the sort of thing that can drive you up your adobe wall. Once it starts there isn't a thing that can be done about it except to put a bucket under the leak. A few ounces of prevention are worth several tons of cure. In other words, build a good roof to start with. You'll keep comfortably dry throughout the heaviest downpour and even while those 4 or 5 inches of accumulated snow melt away in the spring sun.

YOUR ROOF

Even the best constructed roof is not completely permanent. Usually, sometime after the 10th year and before the 20th, leaks begin to develop and repairs have to be made. Sometimes an entirely new roof must be built.

Traditionally, the old adobes were covered with a foot or more of an adobe soil mixture with a heavy clay content. It takes a lot of water and considerable time to get clay soaked through. As long as efficient run-off is provided, no water will seep through such a

Fig. 8-10. An extreme example of what can happen to an adobe building when the roof is not cared for.

thickness of clay-rich adobe. However, like all adobe, water tends to wash it away, small amounts at a time (Figs. 8-10, 8-11 and 8-12). Such a roof will need to be built up again year after year.

Obviously none of us would want to be bothered with such frequent and annoying chores. Therefore, we might as well take advantage of whatever modern materials are available. The most commonly used material is asphalt roofing felt, available in a variety of thicknesses. But because this is also affected by weather, especially sun and heat, it needs to be adequately protected.

Since a good roof is so important and since subsequent repairs tend to be costly and often frustrating, it would seem advisable to have the roof built by a professional roofer. Some of them may be willing to guarantee the integrity of the roof for a reasonable period of time.

Regardless of who does the actual work, a good roof consists of several layers of material:

- The decking, a layer of at least 4-inch insulation material.
- An additional roof deck above the insulation, usually constructed of ½ inch plywood and supported by joists so that it won't compress the insulation material.
- Above that, several layers of roofing felt.
- These should then be topped by gravel. Use light colored in hot desert areas and darker gravel elsewhere. Pour it on

Fig. 8-11. If the roof is not taken care of on an adobe building, it collapses.

top of hot asphalt which, when it hardens, will hold the gravel in place.

The space between the two decking layers that is filled with the insulation material should be vented to the outside. The vents need to be covered with a fine wire screen to prevent birds from building nests in the space.

Gabled Roofs

Gabled roofs, atypical of adobe structures, offer greater areas to be used for insulation. If money is no object, the roofing felt can be covered with and protected by Spanish tile. If properly installed, this tile will produce a roof that will last practically forever. Be sure that the tiles extend far enough outward to avoid the water runoff from leaking down the adobe walls and ruining the plaster.

Fig. 8-12. Once an adobe roof collapses, the building soon becomes a ruin which is beyond saving.

Fig. 8-13. A close look at a small section of the Taos Pueblo shows the small windows and the stubs of the vigas separating the various stories and supporting the roof. It also shows canales which drain the water off the roof far enough from the walls to protect them from excessive water damage.

Fig. 8-14. Icicles are hanging from the canales of this adobe home.

Flat Roofs

Flat roofs, in addition to what has been said earlier, need a *parapet*. A parapet is continuation of the walls above the level of the roof, rising approximately a foot or so. This assures that the water will run off through the canales which must be built into the parapet. They must also extend outward far enough to keep the water run-off

Fig. 8-15. Snow is piled up on the vigas of this adobe home.

clear of the walls (Fig. 8-13). Be sure to place the canales in a place where prolonged run-off and dripping doesn't get in the way of traffic or the view out of a window. When several inches of snow start to melt, water is likely to keep running from these canales for several days. This often freezes at night, producing spectacular icicles (Figs. 8-14, 8-15 and 8-16). The canales are U-shaped metal drains and should be supported by extended vigas or the weight of those icicles will cause them to break off.

ROOF AND CEILING OPTIONS

Chimneys, vent pipes, skylights and the like must be specially treated with flashings of extra heavy roofing felt or metal. This will cause the water to run away from them and not start to gradually leak through the space where they are sticking out through the roof.

Skylights are especially vulnerable to leaks. There is a saying in Santa Fe that there isn't a single skylight in that town (and there are thousands) that doesn't start to leak eventually. The trouble is that once such a leak occurs, the only effective way to stop it is to remove the skylight. It can be put back while the entire section of the roof where it is located is being rebuilt.

I have lived in a house with two such leaking skylights. Over a period of three years the roofer came five times to try and correct

Fig. 8-16. Snow and ice can do extensive damage to an adobe home.

the problem. It never worked. Every time there was a heavy rain or snow started to melt on the roof, we had to cover practically the entire room with plastic sheets because the water would seep into the decking and start to drip in several dozen places at once.

Chapter 9
Entering Your Home

Think of the immediate first impression one gets from walking into a house for the first time. There is something comforting and friendly about walking into a foyer-type space first rather than finding oneself immediately in the living room. It facilitates the greeting of guests and the process of removing overcoats and galoshes. It also prevents outdoor dirt from being dragged all over the house. There should be a fair-sized coat closet with a shelf for hats, gloves and such.

ENTRY HALL

The foyer, or entry hall, doesn't have to be a huge space. It should be large enough for four or five people to greet one another simultaneously. It can lead directly into the living room or it may be separated by bookshelves used as a divider. A row of planters often makes a nice divider also.

In climates with cold winters the foyer also prevents gusts of freezing air from blowing through the living room every time the front door is being opened. In such locations it is imporant to make provisions for a radiator or an outlet for the forced-air heat in the entry hall. This keeps it at a reasonably comfortable temperature even at times when the front door is being opened at frequent intervals, such as might be the case when guests arrive for a party.

A great added convenience, though certainly not a necessity, would be a half bath accessible directly from the entry hall. It keeps

Fig. 9-1. In this home hallways were virtually eliminated by having rooms run into one another, connected by adobe archways.

visitors out of the primary bathrooms and gives women a convenient place to touch up their makeup before being introduced to the other guests.

OTHER HALLWAYS

One typical problem facing the amateur architect in designing his dream house is that he frequently ends up with one or, worse yet, several long hall-ways in his effort to connect all of the individual rooms. A certain amount of hall may be unavoidable, especially if

Fig. 9-2. A relatively narrow hallway can be made pleasant by imaginative decorating.

there are three or more bedrooms and the appropriate number of baths to go with them. But, as a general rule, halls are a waste of space and should be kept to an absolute minimum. Long, narrow halls with doors on either side leading to different rooms tend to result in a hotel effect which is less than desirable. A certain amount of improvement can be achieved by running the hall along an outside wall, with windows on one side and doors leading to the rooms on the other. At least then the hall will be light in the daytime, reducing that unpleasant tunnel effect.

Whenever halls are unavoidable, their dimensions are of significance in making them as pleasant as possible (Fig. 9-1). The absolute minimum width should be not less than 3 feet. It must also be sufficiently wide enough to move furniture in and out. A little extra width, say 4 feet, is a lot better. But don't go over-board. More width becomes a useless waste of space unless you can go all the way to 7 or 8 feet. In that case the hall becomes another room which can be furnished with a chair or two, a cupboard or a chest of drawers and decorated with pictures (Fig. 9-2).

Of course, not all hallways are necessarily ugly or undesirable. One of the more spectacular homes, situated atop a hill in the north section of Santa Fe, is built around a central patio. It is a modern version of the fortress-like homes popular in the early days of the affluent Spaniards. All the way around that inner patio—a thing of beauty in itself with flowers, trees and shrubs—there is an 8 or 10-foot wide passageway.

The patio side of this passageway is glass enclosed with several sliding doors for access. All of the rooms of the house open onto the other side of that passage. In this instance the hall is a thing of beauty, offering easy access to all parts of the house without compromising whatever privacy may be desired.

Chapter 10
Main Living Quarters

No matter what you have done with your hallways, they will eventually lead to several major rooms in your house. Most homes include a living room, a dining area, a kitchen, one or more bedrooms and at least one bathroom.

LIVING ROOM

The living room may not be the primary area for family activities, depending on whether or not your plan also includes a den or family room. One way or the other, the living room can be of any size or shape that appeals to you. However, if the width exceeds 18 or 20 feet, you may have to include some type of structural supports. Wooden pillars or a partial wall could serve as the supports as well as add to the charm of the room. Or a multi-directional fireplace can be built somewhere into the middle of the room, serving the dual purpose of supporting the ceiling and roof as well as providing heat for the room.

Figure 10-1 offers a number of interesting details in its view of an unfinished living room or den. Note the concrete lintel poured above the window and door portion of the right wall. It has been extended across the rear wall and the top of the fireplace. A second bond beam can be seen at the top, supporting the vigas. Electrical wiring has been attached to the wall, but it will eventually be plastered over. Judging by the vents on both sides of the fireplace, it appears to have been constructed with a heatilator type of interior for better distribution of heat. The floor is a solid concrete slab which

Fig. 10-1. The living room is being built in an adobe home.

will probably be covered with either brick, wood or some other floor covering.

You may wish to drop the floor of the living room below the level of the rest of the house (Fig. 10-2) or raise it above that level by a step or two. You may want to combine the room with the primary patio by using sliding double-width glass doors, thus creating the effect of much more space than is actually allotted to the room itself.

Lighting is important both in the daytime when most of the light will be provided by the windows or glass doors and at night when artificial light should create a comfortable and intimate atmosphere. It is certainly advisable to plan dimmers for all electric light in a living

130

Fig. 10-2. Placing different rooms at different levels often provides added charm. Note the use of aged wood in the door and steps. The inside of this adobe wall was covered with only a very thin coat of plaster to retain the adobe-brick look.

room so that the level of available light can be adjusted to fit any particular occasion.

In planning the layout and the best location for the fireplace, think in terms of being able to create groupings of furniture which will permit small numbers of people to carry on a conversation without having to sit on the floor or to shout at each other all the way across the room.

If there is going to be a television set and a stereo system in the room, you might want to think in terms of recesses in the walls for built-in speakers or for the television. Bookshelves, either built-in or separate, are an important consideration. There is something sterile about a room without books, therefore ample wall space must be available to accommodate them.

Also arrange for a space to keep a supply of logs for the fireplace. You don't want to have to run outdoors in the middle of a snowstorm every time a new log is needed. Logs are placed vertically on the base of the fireplace in the kind that are normally used in adobe homes. You will have little trouble starting the fire if you use reasonably dry pinon or juniper logs. On the other hand if you prefer the more conventional type of fireplace in which logs are burned horizontally on a grate, you may want to include a gas outlet to minimize the need for kindling. Kindling tends to be messy and is a real pain.

Thought should also be given to the height of the ceiling. There is something particularly attractive about a high ceiling, but the room has to be large enough. A small room with a too-high ceiling is just as uncomfortable as a very large room with a standard eight-foot ceiling. Remember that a viga ceiling has actually two heights, the distance from the floor to the bottom of the vigas, and the distance to the decking above the vigas. A beautifully executed viga ceiling is an important part of the ambience of such a room, but it must be the right height in order to not be either oppressive or so high as to be out of proportion.

DEN

A den or family room is a nice luxury, especially for those who like to maintain a degree of formality in the living room (Fig. 10-3). The den should be large enough to accommodate all members of the family for joint activities, but it need not rival the living room in size. It might be planned as an extension of the kitchen or dining area separated by planters or a breakfast counter. Or it can be an entirely separate room.

Think in terms of informal comfort for your den. It should be a place to read magazines and keep those which are of lasting value. It can be a place to watch television or listen to music. It should be furnished with informal but comfortable couches and easy chairs (Fig. 10-4), a large coffee table (Fig. 10-5) or several smaller ones and possibly a desk. Lighting should be arranged to provide individual pools of light, preferably on individual dimmers to control the intensity of the light in different portions of the room.

A fireplace would seem to be a virtual must to create that atmosphere of cozy warmth during long winter afternoons and evenings.

Fig. 10-3. A rounded wall for a den is being built for this hillside home. All the construction details are clearly discernible at this stage.

Fig. 10-4. When planning a den, think in terms of informal comfort.

Depending on your personal preference, a den may be square, or round, or triangular or of any other shape that might fit into the floor plan. Less conventional shapes often add a feeling of intimacy. This feeling may be further heightened by dropping the level of the floor a step or two below that of the rest of the house. Consider a brick floor covered with incidental Indian or other rugs and some throw pillows for sitting on the floor.

In the final analysis, what is being done with a den depends to a great degree on a variety of factors:

■ Do you work at home and, if so, do you want to use the den as the place in which to work during the day? If that is the case, it will definitely need to be separate from other rooms in the house.

■ Do you and possibly the rest of the family want to be close by while your wife is busy in the kitchen preparing meals? In that case the idea of building the den as an extension of the kitchen or dining area may be preferred. This also comes in handy if you like the idea of informal meals or snacks in front of the television set.

■ Do you have a hobby of some sort? Some hobbies such as stamp or coin collecting require little space and produce no

Fig. 10-5. An informal couch and a large coffee table offer a relaxing atmosphere in this den.

mess. Others need lots of room, may involve the use of tools and create all manner of unavoidable disorder. Thus, if the den is to also serve as a hobby room, you may want to proportion it in a way which will permit separating one end or corner from the rest of the room by planters, bookshelves or some similar arrangement.

■ Do you have a guest room or will the den occasionally have to accommodate overnight visitors? If that is envisioned, it would again seem preferable to plan it as a separate room which could be closed off. It would also be nice if it wasn't too far away from the nearest bathroom.

KITCHEN

Designing a kitchen would, on the surface, seem to be a cut-and-dried affair. Certain appliances such as a refrigerator, range, oven, sink and dishwasher are basic necessities and of fairly standardized proportions. Appropriate space must be allotted for each. Standard counter tops are 25 inches in width, plus about 1 inch for the splash guard along the back.

But remember that whoever does most of the cooking in the family will most likely spend a great deal of time in the kitchen. It should therefore be efficient, comfortable, attractive and laid out in a way that will minimize the amount of walking needed to get from one appliance to the other.

In addition to the basic appliances there must be cabinets to store dishes, pots, pans and foods. In most standard kitchens some of these cabinets tend to have shelves which are too high to be reached by a woman of average height without climbing on a footstool. They are useless except for the storage of items which are used most infrequently.

In trying to work out a practical layout for a kitchen, first decide on the type of appliances you will want to use. Does a standard range with one or two ovens underneath suit your taste? Or would you rather have the ovens built into the wall where they can be placed at a more convenient level? Refrigerators can have doors opening in either direction or have two doors. If you already have a good refrigerator, then the direction in which its door opens must be taken into consideration.

Many families like their kitchens to be open to the dining area or the living room. Others prefer them to be separate and closed off with a wall and door. In the latter case you might want to consider an opening in the wall with a sliding door through which dishes and food can be handed into the dining area without the need to constantly walk back and forth. In either case, an exhaust fan and a vent are need to draw kitchen odors and smoke from the kitchen to the outside (Fig. 10-6). Some stoves come with built-in vents which draw the smoke over some sort of charcoal filter and then blow it back into the room. They are to be avoided like the plague, because no matter what is being prepared, the whole house will smell of it.

Quite a few newer adobe homes have what is referred to as an *island kitchen*. (Fig. 10-7). An island is built into the center of what is usually a rather large kitchen area (Fig. 10-8). Quite often they have a built-in oven range and a fairly sizeable workspace (Fig. 10-9). Such an arrangement is particularly attractive and practical when the kitchen area includes the dining room.

Fig. 10-6. Exhaust is provided through a flue which goes through the cabinets above the range.

Fig. 10-7. An island kitchen with the range built into the island. The island also serves as a breakfast counter.

Fig. 10-8. An island kitchen adds to the uniqueness of this adobe home.

Fig. 10-9. In this kitchen, the range and the sink are built into the island.

Do you like to have your breakfast or other meals outdoors on a patio? Do you plan to do a lot of entertaining outside? If so, you'll want to consider the ease or difficulty with which food, dishes and drinks can be brought from the kitchen to the patio (Figs. 10-10 and 10-11). If it requires dragging everything through half of the house, the patio is likely to be ignored most of the time.

Pantries, once very popular, virtually disappeared from the scene in recent years. But they are making a comeback and are a most desirable feature especially in homes which are located some distance from markets and shopping areas. In such locations, the additional storage space provided by a pantry can be a great convenience.

Don't forget a service sink. It is impractical and unappetizing to have to wash out cleaning rags and mops in the kitchen sink. Ideally, the service sink should be in a separate room with storage space for brooms, mops and the like. It could also house the washer and dryer, in which case there has to be a vent to the outside for the dryer.

DINING AREA

The formal dining room seems to be a thing of the past. It was popular during the era when there were cooks and maids to prepare

Fig. 10-10. A small patio directly outside the kitchen makes having breakfast and other meals outdoors an easy pleasure.

Fig. 10-11. The patio should be an easy walk from the kitchen.

and serve the meals and when families dressed for dinner, making each meal a formal and festive ocassion. No more. Today we don't normally dine. We simply sit down and eat. The entire process usually takes no more than 30 minutes.

What has developed in place of the dining room is often found at one end of an L-shaped living room. It joins the kitchen where a dining table can be quickly and informally set and meals served with a minimum of fuss. There is nothing wrong with this, but if space and budget permit, a separate dining room can be a beautiful luxury to have.

Fig. 10-12. This dining area is next to the island kitchen and features a small corner fireplace.

If you decide to include such a room in your plans don't forget that it requires appropriate furnishings to gain a graceful setting for dinner parties which will certainly be its primary purpose. You need a large and elegant dining table with chairs to match. There should be sideboards, preferably glass-fronted, to hold the better china and crystal. End tables or cupboards are also handy additions.

Lighting is important. There should be enough light to see what is being eaten, yet too much light will ruin the atmosphere. You may like eating by candle light, but even then a certain amount of extra illumination will be necessary. Usually a candelabra of some design which fits into the overall decor is an ideal solution. Put it on a dimmer to be able to control the amount of light you may want at any given time.

Logically the dining room should be next to the kitchen (Fig. 10-12). If the appropriate wall space is available, an opening in the wall through which dishes and food can be handed from the kitchen into the dining room is a great convenience. It should be equipped with shelf space on either side and with a sliding or other type of door which can be closed when the opening is not in use.

As a general rule the desired formality of such a dining room will be enhanced if the floor is of high quality hardwood. Such a floor gives a feeling of warmth and elegance. And it is relatively easy to keep clean. Rugs are a poor idea in dining areas because it is virtually impossible to prevent food from occasionally falling on the floor, causing rugs to become spotted and stained.

Unlike other rooms, a formal dining room can rarely be used for any other purpose. Therefore, unless you are in the habit of serving formal dinners or giving dinner parties with considerable frequency, the room is likely to be used infrequently. But don't think that simply because it will rarely be used, it might as well take up as little space as possible. Too small a dining room defeats the purpose for which it is planned. The whole idea of festive formality requires ample space. A proportion of 12 by 15 feet would seem to be about right, unless the planned parties are quite large. That would require a longer, though not necessarily wider room.

Windows are relatively unimportant, considering that the room will nearly always be used with artificial light. One window on the narrow wall should suffice to provide light in the daytime and the ventilation needed to clear out food odors. With plenty of wall space left over, this might be an ideal place in which to hang valuable paintings.

BEDROOMS

How many bedrooms will you need? First of all, there is the so-called master bedroom for you and your wife. There should be a second bedroom even if the family only consists of the two of you, just in case one of you comes down with a bad cold and you want to save the unaffected spouse from catching it. Such a second bedroom might double as a study, reading or sewing room. In that case, the bed itself should probably be one of those convertible sofas. An additional advantage of such a second room is that it can be used as a guest room, if a separate guest room is not part of your plan.

Fig. 10-13. A fireplace in the bedroom is a pleasant luxury.

In additon, if there are children, they too need room in which to sleep, play and work. Ideally, each should have his or her own room because privacy becomes increasingly important as they grow older. The number of children in your family and the available budget will definitely affect your decision.

Let's take one bedroom at a time.

The Master Bedroom

The variety of preferences when it comes to the place to sleep is virtually unlimited. Some people like a relatively small room with

Fig. 10-14. A double door leads from the bedroom to a small patio area.

just enough space for a bed, the necessary chest of drawers and ample closet space. Others prefer to wake up in a large room, comfortably furnished with easy chairs, a sofa, incidental tables and possibly a fireplace in which the ashes from last night's fire are still glowing (Fig. 10-13). Still others like to build a mezzanine type of area above part of the living room and use it for sleeping. Or one might consider a small private patio outside the master bedroom with large sliding glass doors to be able to enjoy the view of the early morning sun on the trees and shrubs (Fig. 10-14).

Regardless of personal preferences as to size, shape and location, certain basic requirements are an absolute must. Ample closet space is one. Preferably one entire wall should be set aisde as a closet with sliding doors. There must also be drawer space, either built-in or separate. The latter requires an adequate amount of uninterrupted wall space to accommodate the chests. On either side of the bed there should be room for a night table and lamp. What about a dressing room? You may want to use part of the bedroom as a place for a dressing table with a mirror and space for cosmetics and such. Or you may want to plan a separate small room for this purpose (Fig. 10-15). Either way, it will help to reduce congestion in the bathroom (Fig. 10-16).

Fig. 10-15. A separate dressing area is a desirable feature. Here light is provided by a skylight, since there are no other windows.

Fig. 10-16. Your bathroom will remain less congested if you have a separate dressing room.

A certain amount of care should be exercised in planning the location of windows and glass doors. Do you like to sleep with curtains drawn or open? If you prefer opaque curtains which keep the room dark no matter what is going on outside, then the placement of the windows and doors is not too critical. On the other hand, it you like to keep your curtains and windows open at night, you don't want windows located in such a way that the early morning sun shines right into your face while you're trying to snatch another 30 minutes of sleep. It's a nice feeling to have the sun shine into the room as long as it doesn't act as an alarm clock which can't be turned off.

Fig. 10-17. Ceramic walls accent this stall shower.

Second Bedroom

If the second bedroom is planned as nothing more than a second bedroom, then it will probably see little use except when you have overnight guests, one of you is sick or you have reached the stage in your life where you and your wife decide that sleeping in separate rooms is, after all, more restful. The rest of the time it is likely to develop into a place where things that have more or less outlived their usefulness will be stashed, especially if there is no practical storage space elsewhere. If that is the kind of room it is, all it needs is a closet of a reasonable size, a space for a chest of drawers, a chair or two, a night table, lamp and of course a bed.

Assuming that the available square footage is limited, it would seem more intelligent to plan this room as a combination second bedroom and study, library or hobby room. While even then it can still be fairly small, there should be room for comfortable chairs, a coffee table and possibly a desk of some kind. If it is to be used as a study or reading room, a small corner fireplace might be a desirable feature.

While a room like this would not necessarily require a direct access to its own bath, it should be located reasonably close to one because if and when it doubles as a guest room, it would be unpleasant for the guests to have to wander all over the house on their way to and from the bathroom.

Children's Rooms

Children's requirements tend to vary considerably from individual to individual. They also change as they grow older. As a general rule it is best to plan these rooms to be of a fairly good size, with as many built-in closets and storage spaces as possible. They should be uncluttered in design with plenty of window area for ample light. There has to be room for a single bed (or several, if the room is to be shared), several chairs, a table and possibly a desk and either built-in or separate shelves for books. Since children in their early years tend to be messy, a linoleum or other easy-to-maintain floor is usually the most practical choice. Walls should be finished in some sort of washable surface such as latex paint or washable wallpaper.

In addition children are often quite noisy. It is therefore a good idea to plan the location of their rooms as far away from the rest of the house as possible. Since there should be a separate bathroom for them, this may require some extra expense in terms of plumbing. However, the resulting peace and quiet for the grown-up faction is certainly worth the additional cost.

Guest Houses

The idea of a separate guest house, though certainly a luxury, is becoming increasingly popular. The advantages are numerous. First of all, if used for guests, it provides them with privacy and keeps them from being constantly underfoot. This makes the idea of a prolonged stay less painful for all concerned. Secondly, if by some happenstance a time should come when money is tight, guest houses can often be rented for sufficient amounts of money that may cover part or all of the mortgage payments. In future years when the children are gone and you may feel uncomfortable rambling around all alone in a huge house, you may want to move into the guest house yourself and rent the main house. That rental could provide you with a nice little extra income.

Ideally a guest house should contain a small bedroom, a living room with a small eating area, either a kitchenette or a small kitchen and a bathroom. In some areas zoning restrictions make it illegal to include a full kitchen in guest houses on the assumption that this would constitute a multiple dwelling. However, there are usually ways to circumvent such a regulation by adding some kind of kitchen facility after the guest house has been built.

When space permits it is a nice idea to design the outdoor space and plantings in such a way that the guest house ends up with its own

Fig. 10-18. A ceramic-tiled stall shower adds to the uniqueness of this bathroom.

reasonably private patio. That way, if you do ever find that you want to rent it, or live there and rent the main house, a degree of privacy is maintained for both. In this context there should also be a driveway leading directly to the guest house. Possibly it could even include some sort of covered car port.

Don't forget some means of heating the place. A fireplace might suffice in areas with mild winters, but elsewhere some type of gas, oil or electric heating unit is essential.

BATHROOMS

Most bathrooms are strictly utilitarian, containing a tub and, or shower, sink, toilet and just enough space for one person to do the various things which are supposed to be done in a bathroom. For most bathrooms that is just fine, but when it comes to the master bath, how about letting your fantasies run rampant?

Stall Shower. How about a stall shower with walls of ceramic tile (Figs. 10-17 and 10-18) and two showerheads? One could be high enough to stand under it upright and the other could be at a level which permits taking a shower while keeping your hair dry. A stall shower like that should be roughly 3 by 3 feet, although a few inches less would be acceptable. Making it much larger makes little sense, unless you like to shower with a friend.

Bathtub. Maybe you find a standard tub boring. If so, a sunken tub, designed to dimensions of your own preference and possibly lined with ceramic tile, might add a touch of elegance to the room. It can be rectangular, round or any shape that turns you on (Fig. 10-19). It can be large enough to let you lie in it full length, in which case the width should be just right to permit sitting up with the feet propped against the other side.

The Sink. Do you like an individual sink, free standing on a pedestal, or do you prefer pullman-type sinks set into a large surface area with a row of cabinets underneath (Figs. 10-20 and 10-21)? The latter is usually more practical, although some people like the former from a point of view of esthetics. Regardless of which you prefer, there should be provisions for a medicine cabinet, preferably built into the wall and a large mirror. Another mirror on the opposite wall would permit seeing oneself from both front and back. To accomplish this the two mirrors can't be exactly parallel. They have to be at a slight angle to one another. Walls in adobe houses tend to be slightly crooked anyway so this should present no major problem. Alternately, one might be hinged.

The Toilet. Regardless of whether you choose the cheaper small type or the more expensive larger version, the overall space

Fig. 10-19. If you find a standard tub boring, be creative with yours.

into which a toilet is placed should be not less than 3 by 4 feet. And while you're at it, put the toilet paper someplace where it can be reached without the need for major contortions.

Colors. Bathroom fixtures come in a wide variety of colors, but it should be remembered that those colors cannot be changed. If sink, toilet and tub are blue, you'll be stuck with that color and everything else in the room will always have to complement it. Unless you're absolutely certain that a certain basic color is what you'll be happy with for years to come, white fixtures might be a better idea. Then whatever color is used will be in terms of wall and ceiling paint, wallpaper and decorative details, all of which can be changed.

Fig. 10-20. Sinks are often set into a large surface area with a row of cabinets underneath.

Windows. Most builders seem to take it for granted that a bathroom window should be one of those tiny things. This is probably a hangover from building in cities where you wouldn't want your neighbor to look in from next door while you're doing your thing. But if there is no next door neighbor, a large window with a view of the outside would seem to be preferred.

One of the most sensational bathrooms I have ever seen had one entire glass wall with a sliding glass door looking out onto a small, fully enclosed patio. Since that patio was inaccessible from any direction other than the bathroom, complete privacy was preserved,

Fig. 10-21. When it comes to designing a bathroom, why not let your imagination run wild?

while at the same time, the feeling was created that one was taking a bath out in the garden.

On the practical side, don't forget that a bathroom needs a vent with an exhaust fan. It is also a good idea to arrange for some sort of special heating system because usually a great deal of time is spent in the bathroom in the early morning hours before the house has had a chance to get warm.

Chapter 11
Hobby Rooms

Anyone who would even consider the do-it-yourself aspect of building an adobe home is likely to be the kind of person who needs a place in which to work with his hands. Once the house itself is nearing completion, he may want to build bookshelves, make his own furniture or indulge in such hobbies as painting, sculpting or even building a model railroad layout. Regardless of what leisure time activity appeals to him, it is likely to involve the use of tools. This will result in noise and a certain amount of mess.

WORKSHOPS

Neither the living room nor the den are suitable for this sort of activity. Thus, a workshop or hobby room is probably of greater importance than one might initially think. If it is to be part of the house itself, try to place it as far away from the primary living portion of the house as possible. This will minimize the annoyance created when noisy power tools are being used. A simple cement slab floor is damage resistant and easy to clean. It is therefore preferred to wood, vinyl tile, brick or linoleum. Walls of raw wood, possibly with the studs exposed, simplify the task of storing tools within easy reach and of constructing utility shelves.

If an enclosed garage is part of the plan, it might be sensible to consider to enlarge it sufficiently to incorporate such a hobby room and workshop. This automatically helps to remove the noise and mess from the main house. But remember to include a means of heating the room if you want it to be usable throughout the winter months. The need for access to electricity goes without saying. You may also want to consider installing a sink and water faucet if the kind of work which you anticipate doing involves the use of water, even if only for the purpose of cleaning.

What size should such a room be? That depends entirely on what the planned activities involve. If you are hankering to construct massive pieces of furniture, you'll obviously need ample space. The final decision will probably be a compromise between what you'd like to have and what can be accommodated within the available space. Remember that such a workshop does not necessarily have to adhere to conventional room proportions. For example, if it is located in the back of a two-car garage, you may end up with a 20-foot long and 6- or 7-foot wide sausage of a room which may seem strange at first, but will actually prove to be very workable.

Don't forget to include windows. Not only are they needed to provide ample light, but even more important is the ventilation. No matter what you'll be doing in there, sooner or later you'll be using paints, or lacquer or some other material producing noxious odors. This will require easy access to a lot of fresh air. If a regular window is impossible for some reason, you may want to consider an openable skylight. Such skylights are equipped with a heavy-duty steel spring. They can be opened and closed easily from the inside and are commercially available. When properly installed they don't present any leakage problems. If none of this is possible, a vent with a reasonably powerful exhaust fan may suffice, but then all work will have to be done by artificial light.

STUDIOS AS WORKSHOPS

The workshop of an artist is a studio and since artists seem to be particularly drawn to the peculiar charm of adobe buildings, a brief section on the requirements for a studio seems indicated.

We might first analyze the different kinds of studios appropriate to various types of art forms. A sculptor's requirements tend to differ somewhat from those of a painter or a photographer. A musician will have still other needs.

A PAINTER'S STUDIO

Most painters like to work in a studio with a northern exposure, with large window areas giving ample indirect light, but no direct sunlight (Fig. 11-1). The size of such a studio room will depend largely on the type of painting being done. If the artist frequently works on huge canvasses or on full-size designs for murals, he will need ample space. He will need this space not only to accommodate

Fig. 11-1. Most painters like a studio with large windows facing north.

the painting itself, but also so that he can step back and examine his work from an appropriate distance and perspective. On the other hand, if he prefers working on a small scale, less room may be needed.

In either case, if live models are frequently used, the studio should include a small dressing room and adequate space for the model to pose. In that case it is preferred to have the studio located in a way which permits direct access from the outside. Then models won't have to go through the family living area in order to get to it.

Most such studios with their large windows and often high ceilings will be harder to heat than the average room. Provisions should be made to direct ample heat into the studio to keep it a comfortable place in which to work during the cold season. An additional convenience would be a half bath which includes a sink and toilet. The sink comes in handy to wash brushes and the like and the toilet keeps both the artists and the model within the confines of the studio.

The floor is a problem. A concrete slab would seem easiest to clean, but it tends to be hard on the feet for the artist who is likely to spend hours standing in front of his easel. A wood or other more resilient floor is more comfortable and gives a feeling of warmth. A good solution might be a wood or adobe-mud floor with some type of washable linoleum covering in the portion of the room where paints are likely to drip on the floor.

A PHOTOGRAPHER'S STUDIO

A photographer has different requirements. Most prefer to work with artificial light, so windows are unimportant. If they are included, the should be equipped with shutters to cut out all daylight when necessary. In most instances such a studio will have to be quite large and include ample storage spaces for props, backdrops and the like. The walls should be of smooth plaster or a similar surface, painted white to reflect light. The floor should be smooth to simplify the task of moving lights and camera tripods.

If models are used, the studio should be located to permit direct access from the outside. There will also have to be a dressing room with space for a makeup table and a rod to hang clothes.

In addition there has to be provisions for a darkroom. This includes plumbing, large sinks for the developing trays and place for an enlarger. Since this room has no window and is otherwise light tight, it will need some means of ventilation. It may also require an air conditioning unit in order to be usable during the hot summer months.

With the plumbing already in place, a half bath or possibly a three-quarter bath should certainly be part of the plan.

A SCULPTOR'S STUDIO

A sculptor's requirements tend to parallel those of a painter as far as light, northern exposure and overall size are concerned. He, too, will need access to water, a place for models to dress or undress and the necessary means of heating or cooling the place.

There are certain aspects in which the sculptor's requirements differ. Many of a sculptor's raw materials, such as marble, rock and metal are heavy and cumbersome to transport. While there seems to be no reason why a painter's or photographer's studio could not be on an upstairs level, a sculptor must not only consider that the floor of his studio will have to be firm enough to carry considerable weights, he will also need a means of backing a truck or van right up to the studio door in order to bring his materials into the studio. The finished work will be loaded onto a truck or trailer for transportation to the gallery or exhibition.

A MUSICIAN'S STUDIO

Here we are dealing with acoustics rather than light and the question of what to do with live models. The size of the room, its shape and wall surfaces determine the character of the sound produced by instruments or song. Smooth hard surfaces on walls and ceilings will tend to produce an echoing tunnel effect which will be annoying to the artist and make recording any kind of sound virtually impossible. A certain amount of curtains and hangings will help to minimize that effect, but too much could result in dead sound which is equally undesirable.

A room with a multitude of corners, angles and parallel walls where sound can bounce back and forth frequently results in a very respectable sound quality.

In order to protect family and neighbors from being exposed to hours of practicing music, the studio should most probably be sound-proofed. If all walls are of adobe and of adequate thickness, that should take care of it. On the other hand, stud walls may need special soundproofing. The same will hold true for doors which lead directly from the studio to the living quarters. This soundproofing works in two ways. It not only keeps the music inside the studio, but it also prevents traffic and other disturbing noises from bothering the musicians.

The ideal size for such a studio depends on the use to which it will be put. There may have to be space and access for a grand piano.

If several musicians will frequently gather for group practice, the space must be sufficient for all of them. If test recordings are to be made, the quality of the sound is of greater importance than it would be otherwise.

With efficient soundproofing resulting in a room which is hermetically sealed, silent ventilation, heating and air conditioning become an important and necessary feature.

Obviously a great deal of thought should go into the planning of a studio. Many hours will be spent there so it is well worth the time and expense to do it right from the outset.

Chapter 12
Areas of Moderate Dimensions

These are the spaces which are necessary, yet are frequently overlooked by the do-it-yourself home designer.

UTILITY SPACES

What we're talking about here is room for the washer and dryer, the water heater, the central heating unit and a service sink. Let's take one at a time.

Washer and Dryer

Washers and dryers are relatively standard in size, measuring around 30 by 30 inches each. The washer requires attachments to the hot and cold water line, a drain leading to the sewer or septic tank and preferably a floor drain to minimze the danger of flooding the place if it ever overflows. Keep in mind that most washers will do that at one time or another.

The dryer may either be gas or electric. If it is a gas dryer, it needs access to the gas line. Furthermore it needs to be vented to the outside.

Most professional builders will habitually place the washer and dryer in a place which backs up to either the kitchen or a bathroom, thus reducing the need for additional plumbing. But a few dozen feet of additional plumbing are a relatively small item if you feel that a different location would be preferable. By all means think in terms of convenience rather than the saving of a few dollars.

A good proportion for a room for a side-by-side washer and dryer would be about 3½ by 5½ feet. Westinghouse produces a front-loading washer with the dryer mounted on top, designed primarily for apartments and mobile homes. (The identical unit is sold by Montgomery Ward under its own label.) By using one of these units the space requirement can be cut in half.

Water Heater

Water heaters come in varying capacities. Since the cost for a larger one is not a great deal higher than that for one with less capacity, it is certainly advisable to opt for one of sufficient size that will permit several members of the family to take showers without having to wait until sufficient hot water is again available.

When at all possible it is to be preferred to locate the heater reasonably close to where the hot water is being used. That way the time it takes until hot water is available at the tap is reduced to a minimum. Be sure that the hot and cold water pipes are not placed so close to one another that the temperature of one affects that of the other. Otherwise you're likely to end up with warm water coming out of the cold faucet. This can be annoying every time you turn on the tap to get a glass of cold water to drink.

Keep in mind that water heaters have been known to spring a leak or even to burst. This could result in expensive damage to floors, carpets, and furniture. For this reason it might be worth considering locating it in a space which is outside the main house. If that doesn't work, drop the level of the floor in its space a foot or so below the adjoining floor levels and incorporate a floor drain.

If the heater uses gas, a gas line will also have to be provided.

Central Heating

If it is at all possible to include a partial basement or even an adequate crawl space under the house, then that is the ideal place for the heating unit. If that is not feasible, a space must be found somewhere in the house. Provisions must then be made for the air ducts through which the air circulates to and from each room in the house.

The type of construction generally associated with adobe building often makes it difficult to find a logical place for all of these ducts. Where that is the case, a different type of central heating may have to be considered. The easiest to install are electric heating units which are placed along the floorboards. They take up virtually no room, require no structural consideration and are totally silent. Their drawback is that it takes a long time to heat a cold room and the cost of operation is fairly high. An alternate system involves circulating hot water through radiators or a network of thin copper pipes embedded in the floor. With this system the cost of the initial installation is quite high and it also takes longer to obtain adequate heat than with forced air. On the other hand, it is silent and the overall effect is most pleasant. It does require a second and separate water heater which might best be placed alongside the other water heater where provision for drainage and protection from water damage has already been made.

Service Sink

The service sink has already been mentioned in the chapter about kitchens. It is best located in a small, separate space adjoining the kitchen or pantry. It should include a door to the outside. Such a space can also be used for the storage of brooms, mops, cleaning rags and the like. If large enough it might also serve to contain a small supply of fireplace logs and protect them from rain and snow. A bare cement floor is to be preferred here because it will be unaffected by unavoidable water spillage.

Fig. 12-1. When the garage becomes a storage space, the cars are left out in the weather.

CLOSETS

In the long run there are few greater annoyances associated with living in any given house than a lack of closet and storage space. Living invariably involves the gradual accumulation of all sorts of things which even if not in daily use, one will want to keep. No matter what the number and size of closets and storage spaces, they always end up being filled to the brim. As soon as that happens most of us start taking things out to the garage and before we know it the car is left out in the rain and snow (Fig. 12-1).

The trouble is that such spaces take up a fair amount of square footage. Each square foot costs as much to build as any other, regardless of its eventual use. As a result we tend to shy away from alotting too much square footage to dead space (Fig. 12-2). Unless you are one of those rare birds who throws everything away the moment it has outlived its immediate usefulness, this is false economy.

There are different types of basic closets which are an absolute necessity. Each bedroom must have sufficient closet space for the clothes of the occupants of that room. Such closets must be 2 feet deep in order to accommodate suits and dresses on hangers without crushing them. If the closet is of the walk-in type, 6 feet is an ideal width. It provides for 2 feet of hanging space on each side and 2 feet of walking space. If only 4 feet are available, only one rod can be installed on one side of the closet (Fig. 12-3).

Shelves should be installed above the rod to hold suitcases, handbags, hats and whatever. A low shelf might be useful for shoes. One might also consider two rods, one below the other, to hang blouses, sweaters and jackets which do not require the full length from the upper rod to the floor.

The most practical type of closet door is a sliding door. They come in a variety of sizes, are relatively cheap and fairly easy to install. In addition, they don't use up space in the bedroom when left open.

Other necessary closets are a 2-foot deep coat closet in the entry hall and a linen closet. The latter should contain shelves and be large enough to hold linens, sheets and towels in such a way that permits taking them out without having to lift up a dozen sheets in order to get at a dish towel or face cloth. The contents of linen closets tend to be used in various parts of the house including bathrooms, bedrooms, the kitchen area and the dining area. They are often located somewhere in a hall, more or less equidistant from all parts of the house.

Fig. 12-2. The thickness of double-brick adobe walls permits the building-in of shelves and alcoves to display whatever we like to keep in full view.

167

Fig. 12-3. A large walk-in closet with a skylight is likely to be the delight of the lady of the house.

So much for the absolute necessities. But what do we do with old records, toys no longer in use, tools, skis, roller or ice-skates, and all the 101 diverse belongings which we rarely use but don't want to get rid of? If a regular garage is part of the plan, storage cabinets can be built-in. There will be more about that in a later chapter. If all you're planning on is an open carport, that will be a less than satisfactory location in which to store anyting worth storing at all.

The basements and attics of conventional houses traditionally served as ideal depositories for things one wanted to keep. After generations of use many attics have proven to be a veritable treasury of family history. But adobe houses are usually built directly on firm ground with no basement or even a crawl space and the flat roof makes an attic impossible. For this reason some type of large storage space must be planned for as part of the house itself. If there are stairs, the space underneath them might suffice. If not and if no other suitable area can be set aside, you might just consider a lean-to against one of the outer walls. If constructed of adobe and properly porportioned, it can be made to look quite attractive by giving the impression that it is an integral part of the house itself.

Children's rooms need more than the average amount of closet and storage space. While the clothes closet may not need to be as large as that for adults, they do need space for toys, school books, tools, baseball gloves, football helmets and the million and a half other things that they will accumulate and cherish.

Chapter 13
Fireplaces

An adobe home without fireplaces is like life without love. Something vital is missing. You will notice that I said fireplaces, plural. Much of the charm of older adobes results from the fact that there are fireplaces in practically every room. A fireplace is the focal point of any room (Fig. 13-1). It is its heart and soul, radiating a feeling of warmth and welcome to all who enter (Fig. 13-2).

Include as many fireplaces as you can afford in your original plan. If for some reason or other you can't or don't want to build all of them right away, be sure to pour adequate foundations wherever a fireplace might be built sometime in the future. It is necessary that fireplaces be planned for and preferably built during the early stages of construction because they require special consideration with reference to the strength and thickness of the foundation. The one in Fig. 13-3 is apparently ready to be tested. The adobe bricks in the foreground will be used in the construction of interior walls. Note the nailing blocks embedded in the wall at the left. They will eventually be used to hold a door frame.

Where should your fireplaces be? The living room and den are obvious candidates. A fireplace in the master bedroom is also a desirable feature. You may even consider putting one in the kitchen (Fig. 13-4) where it can be used in the winter to broil steaks on a hibachi.

There are two basic types of fireplaces. One is the conventional type. It is placed flat against or into a wall. The other, traditional in adobe homes, is the corner fireplace (Fig. 13-5). This latter type is

Fig. 13-1. An adobe fireplace built flush into a wall in an adobe home.

simpler to construct because two of its walls are already in existence. When no corner is available a *padercita,* a short piece of wall, can be built into the room. This creates a corner for a fireplace while at the same time serves to divide the room into several areas of activity (Figs. 13-6 and 13-7). A third possibility, although relatively rarely found, is a free-standing fireplace in the middle of the room (Fig. 13-8). There are commercially available ready-made Swedish fireplaces or one can be sculpted out of adobe (Figs. 13-9 and 13-10).

The size of a fireplace should be in a sensible relation to the size of the room. A huge fireplace in a small room will tend to look as much out of place as would a small one in a large living room. From a practical point of view with an eye toward the amount of heat it will generate, the size is of less importance than one might think. I have seen quite small ones put out a great deal of warmth and huge ones which didn't seem to do much at all.

The fact remains that a fireplace is more important from the point of view of the esthetic pleasure it provides than as means of heating the house. Fireplaces, no matter how well constructed, are always inefficient sources of heat because an excessive percentage of the warmth they produce goes right up the chimney. With this in mind, design your fireplaces for the pleasure they will give and depend on an efficient heating system for warmth.

The traditional Indian fireplace was simply a firebox in the corner of the room with a straight chimney above it to draw out the

172

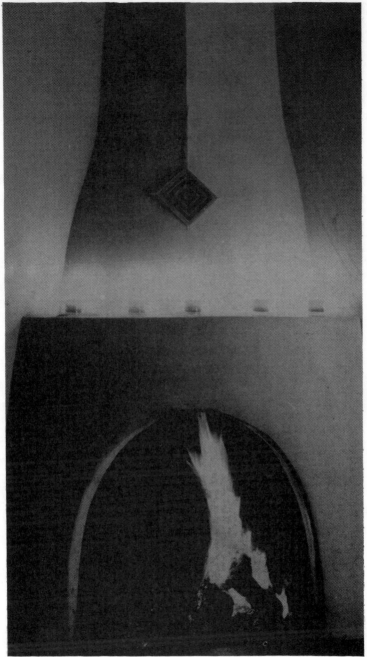

Fig. 13.2. In its stark simplicity a beautifully designed and executed corner fireplace in a remodeled old adobe.

Fig. 13-3. Fireplaces must be planned for and built during the early stages of construction.

Fig. 13-4. A corner fireplace in the part of the kitchen used as a dining area.

Fig. 13-5. A beautifully designed and executed traditional corner fireplace. It can be left with the brick design exposed or it can eventually be plastered over along with the rest of the walls.

smoke. While simple to construct, it is extremely inefficient as far as heat generation is concerned. It is also subject to sudden downdrafts which tend to blow ashes and glowing cinders all over the room.

An efficient modern fireplace (Fig. 13-11) consists of the following:

- foundation
- stem
- throat
- smoke shelf
- flue
- shell
- face
- hearth

Let's take them one at a time.

FOUNDATION

A fireplace is a great amount of weight concentrated in a small area. For this reason it will require a foundation of greater strength than is needed for other portions of the house. The average founda-

Fig. 13-6. A traditional corner fireplace built against a corner formed by one wall and one padercita.

Fig. 13-8. A free-standing fireplace partially completed in an adobe home under construction.

tion for a fireplace is a concrete slab. It is at least 1 foot thick and 4 to 6 inches larger than the actual fireplace. It must be reinforced with rebars and should rest on undisturbed ground. When in doubt, more foundation is always better than less. It would be rather disconcerting to discover after several years that the whole structure is beginning to lean and in danger of tipping over. As already mentioned, while you're in the process of pouring foundations for the whole house, include fireplace foundations in any place in which you can possibly envision that you might eventually want to add a fireplace. At that point the added cost is minimal, whereas if you have to start from scratch and pour an additional foundation later on, it might prove to be a complicated and expensive undertaking.

STEM

This is a masonry structure. It usually consists of concrete blocks which rise from the foundation to the base of the firebox. If the firebox is to be level with the foundation, no stem is needed. If it is to be raised above the level of the foundation, that is where the stem comes in. It is generally a solid construction with all crevices filled with mortar. An opening can be provided for an ash dump with a

Fig. 13-7. An unusual fireplace built against a shallow recess in the adobe wall.

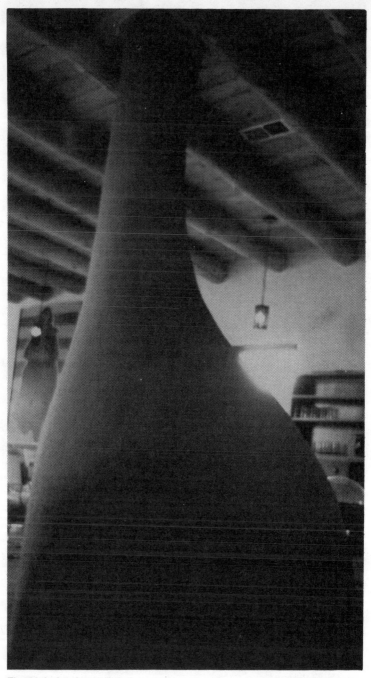

Fig. 13-9. An elegant free-form fireplace in a Santa Fe restaurant.

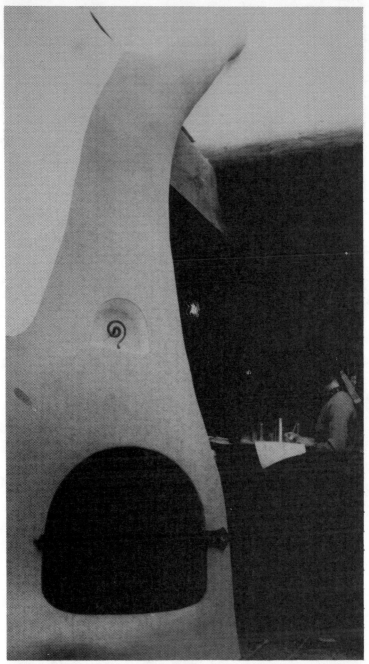

Fig. 13-10. A second view of a unique free-form fireplace in a restaurant in Santa Fe.

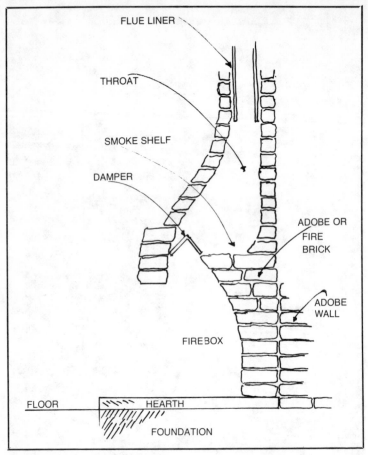

Fig. 13-11. Components of a fireplace.

means of removing the ashes from the outside. This is assuming that the fireplace is built against an outside wall. The height of the stem is not limited and if a fireplace is to be built into an upstairs room, the stem will obviously have to reach all the way up to the second floor.

FIREBOX

This is where your fires are going to be burning. It can be constructed of adobe brick or firebrick. Firebrick is mortared with fireclay or refractory cement. In some areas building codes required firebrick rather than adobe.

The trouble with adobe is that the mud plaster has a tendency to eventually crack away in chunks, requiring a replastering job from time to time.

The back wall of the firebox may be a continuous curve or it may be simply vertical for about a foot or so and then slant toward the room. This provides an angled surface which helps to deflect heat into the room. The side walls should be similarly angled to reflect warmth.

Since the opening of the firebox is what you'll be looking at, its shape should be pleasing. It may be a half oval, as is often the case with corner fireplaces, or a part of an oval with the top cut straight across or it can be rectangular, as is usually the case with conventional fireplaces built into the middle of a wall. In order to efficiently build symmetrical curved openings, you may find that it is useful to cut a template from a piece of plywood and then build the opening around that template.

THROAT

This is the upper portion of the firebox. It tapers to support the damper. You can buy prefabricated throats which simplify construction or it can be made of firebrick or adobe that is laid in such a fashion that each layer of brick extends beyond the edge of the one below it. This is called *corbelling*.

If a prefabricated metal throat is used it is important that there be a space between the metal surfaces and the brick. It should be insulated with fiberglass or rockwool. Any brick which actually touches the metal is in danger of being pushed out of place or cracked as the metal expands in the heat.

SMOKE SHELF

This is a necessary feature in the construction of any fireplace. It prevents downdrafts from reaching the firebox and blowing ashes or cinders into the room. In older fireplaces that were built without this feature, a stove-pipe damper often had to be inserted in the flue. When closed, this would prevent wind from blowing down the chimney. However, since it had to be open when the fireplace was in use, its usefulness was limited not to mention that fact that practically all the heat simply went up and out of the chimney.

FLUE

The simplest means of building the flue is to use clay-tile flue liners of the appropriate size. This results in a minimum number of joints and is cheaper than building the whole thing out of brick. It should be encased in brick and must be built up to extend at least 2 feet or more above the roof. Once the flue has been installed, it is a good idea to make a fire in the firebox and test the entire system to make sure that it works and draws all right.

SHELL

The shell is the main structure which surrounds the basic firebox and which can be built to any size and shape that seems appealing. Most building codes require a minimum thickness for the shell. It is usually 1 foot if the fireplace is built into a stud wall or if there is any wood adjacent to it. If it is built into an adobe wall, the masonry abode will serve as part of the shell.

The shell can be built of adobe, solid bricks, rocks laid in concrete or any other solid masonry material or combination of materials. This choice will depend on the requirements of the prevailing local building codes.

FACE

The face is strictly decorative and has nothing to do with the basic fireplace structure. It can be adobe plaster that is smoothed by hand to give it that slightly undulating effect—part of the charm of working with adobe. It can be brick, rough-hewn rocks, marble or any other non-flammable material. Whatever material is decided upon, take your time. This final result is supposed to be a thing of beauty, so don't mess it up by doing sloppy work in a hurry.

Virtually every fireplace face will include some kind of mantel. The sculpted adobe corner fireplaces usually simply have a narrow shelf built-in roughly at the level of the damper installation. Others may have wooden shelves projecting from the face. In this latter case, be sure to remember to build adequate supports deep enough into the face and possibly shell to support not only the shelf itself, but also anything that may eventually be placed on it.

HEARTH

A hearth is simply a projection of non-flammable material at the level of the base of the firebox. Its purpose is to catch sparks and prevent them from falling on flammable surfaces such as wooden floors or carpets. It normally extends in front of the firebox for about 1½ feet. If your floors are brick or a concrete slab, no hearth is needed. On the other hand, a raised hearth in front of a fireplace which is built up to the appropriate height may be extended on either side of the firebox, thus providing a pleasant place to sit.

There are prefabricated circulating fireplace structures available on the market such as heatilators. Some include fans which blow the warmed air into the room. In one unit they usually consist of a double-walled metal firebox, damper and throat. Using one of these units makes the job easier for the do-it-yourself builder, but he will be stuck with whatever sizes and dimensions are available. The installation involves building a floor for the firebox on which the unit rests. It will then have to be enclosed in a shell. This shell may have to be larger in order to accommodate the air ducts. As far as cost is concerned, it may come out about even because what is being paid for the prefabricated unit will be saved in other materials and time.

Chapter 14
Outdoor Projects

For some people a home is not complete without the added attractions of a garage, at least one patio, an outdoor barbecue and a swimming pool.

There is no doubt that these luxuries add to the charm and value of your home and some of them may be within closer reach than you think.

THE GARAGE

Considering what automobiles cost these days, it is amazing to realize how many large and expensive houses exist without a garage or even a carport. Leaving the cars outside in all kinds of weather is bound to be detrimental in the long run. In addition, there is the annoyance of getting soaked whenever it's raining or the annoyance of having to scrape ice and snow off of the windshields on cold winter mornings.

A two-car garage should be considered as a necessary minimum these days, not only for your own convenience, but also because it will seriously affect the resale value. Although the idea of selling right now may be the farthest thing from your mind, virtually every house is going to be sold eventually. If space and budget permit, a three-car garage may be even better.

Whichever you decide, make it big. Twenty by 20 feet is considered the standard size for a conventional two-car garage but unless both cars are VWs or other small compacts, that is really too small. First of all, once the car is inside and the doors are closed, you will want to be able to get from one side of the garage to the other without having to climb over the bumpers. You will also want to be able to open the car doors without smashing them into the side of the other car. Secondly, the garage will also be used to keep bicycles, scooters, lawn mowers and the like. With no basement or attic available for this purpose, it will end up being the primary storage space for all kinds of items. It makes little sense to one day find that your driveway looks like a used car lot because there is no room left in the garage.

The floor of a garage should be a concrete slab, a few inches higher than the ground outside so that rainwater won't run into it. Ideally it should be slightly slanted toward the front so that it can be hosed off and the water will run off to the outside. The walls need not be finished unless you plan to include a means of heating it during the winter. As a matter of fact, unfinished stud walls simplify the task of installing hooks or nails from which to hang things.

Since the average hood of a car is only about 40 or so inches from the ground, it might be a good idea to consider building storage cabinets out from the back wall, some 4 feet off of the ground. Though this would necessitate always walking around the back of the cars when trying to get from one side of the garage to the other, it

Fig. 14-1. There should be direct access from the garage to the house.

Fig. 14-2. Assuming the cost of building a garage is beyond the budget, how about a carport?

can provide a huge amount of storage space out of harm's way.

Standard garage doors are either 8 or 16 feet. There is no particular reason why you could not construct your own in any size that turns you on, however. Most drivers prefer one big door to two small ones because it seems to make getting in and out easier. Also, if you should ever decide to install an automatic door-opener, you'll only have to pay for one of them.

The location of the garage with reference to the main house will necessarily depend on the proportion and topography of the lot. Ideally there should be a door leading directly from the garage to the kitchen or some place near it (Fig. 14-1). This will reduce the chore of lugging groceries from the car to where they are needed. If this is not possible and the garage has to be built as a separate unit some distance from the house, then by all means, plan for a covered walk between the two. It simply doesn't make sense to be unable to get from one to the other in a downpour without getting soaked to the skin.

Assuming that the cost of building a real garage is beyond your budget, how about a carport (Fig. 14-2)? All we are talking about here is a few rough-hewn posts and a roof made of plywood and tarpaper or whatever other material seems practical. It should be slanted just enough to assure water run-off. Sides can be covered with bamboo screens or lattice work with creeping plants. Either of these will provide shade and reduce the direct impact of driving rain.

Direct access from the carport to the house is also a desirable feature. Attaching the carport directly to one side of the house reduces structural problems. It has to be a part of the house where there is no window, though because you wouldn't want to look out onto the carport and give the carbon monoxide, generated when starting a car, the opportunity to seep into the inside.

This floor should also be a concrete slab. It should be a few inches higher than the surrounding ground so that it won't be covered with water and mud from rain or melting snow. Don't forget to make provisions for electricity. You wouldn't want to have to stumble around in the dark.

The major drawback of a carport is the fact that it is no good for storage. Even though it is theoretically possible to hang storage cabinets from the roof to a level above the hood of the cars, the fact that they are exposed to all manner of atmospheric conditions, moisture and changes in temperature makes their usefulness rather limited.

PATIOS

One of the primary pleasures of living in the southwestern United States, where most of the building of new adobes takes place these days, is the fact that the climate is inducive to spending much of one's time outdoors. It is therefore of some importance to carefully plan the patio areas at the very beginning when deciding on the orientation of the structure on the lot. Consideration must be given to the prevailing winds, the heat generated by the sun on summer afternoons, the relation of the road and driveway to the patios and, in turn, to a means of providing privacy (Figs. 14-3 and 14-4) and access to and from the different parts of the house.

If at all possible it is often preferred to think in terms of several smaller patio areas rather than one huge one. A patio with a western exposure, expecially if there is a view of the mountains beyond which the sun will set each evening, can be beautiful. But the afternoon sun may heat such a patio to an uncomfortable degree. Therefore, it would require some shade trees to make it livable.

Another one, oriented toward the south and protected against northerly and northwesterly winds by the house itself, will be usable throughout the winter when the air itself may be quite cold, but the rays of the sun are warm enough to sit out and get a tan.

To the east a small patio could be walled in for total privacy. It might connect with the bedroom or bathroom or both, offering a

Fig. 14-3. On the Camino del Monte Sol in Santa Fe a beautifully maintained adobe wall with heavy abutments surrounds an old adobe home and its patio.

191

Fig. 14-4. An outside entrance to the patio is provided by the surrounding adobe walls.

view of the morning light through the window and glass door areas of those two rooms.

The north of the house is often the least ideal for usable outdoor space. It's not bad in the summer but in the winter, with a fair portion of the patio constantly shaded by the house, snow will tend to accumulate and refuse to melt. In addition, one side of the house must be the one where the water drains through the canales from the roof and the northern side of the house is often the one selected for this. It might also serve as the place in which to bury the septic tank and the associated leach field which tends to be responsible for excessively dense and rapid growth of grasses, bushes, shrubs and weeds. If this growth occurs in one of the to-be-lived-in patios, it could result in constant gardening work to keep it from becoming unmanageable.

Depending on the location of your lot with reference to neighbors, roads and the like, you may wish to enclose the entire lot, including all patios, with an adobe wall (Figs. 14-5 and 14-6). If equipped with a gate which can be closed, this not only assures total privacy, but is also useful in keeping small children from straying into the street. In addition it prevents the dog from running around loose and getting into all kinds of mischief.

Fig. 14-5. An adobe-brick wall provides privacy for a home in the downtown area of Santa Fe.

Fig. 14-6. Privacy is offered to the home by adobe walls surrounding the patio.

Fig. 14-7. Patios come in all shapes and sizes. This one is covered with flagstones.

194

Fig. 14-8. This patio area is distinguished by imaginative wall sections.

195

Fig. 14-9. This small patio is enclosed near the entrance door.

Always consider the view if there is any. A 6-foot or higher wall will tend to effectively cut off whatever view there might be. It is therefore up to you to decide in which direction you will want to compromise.

Patios may include lawns, areas covered with flagstone (Fig. 14-7), gravel walks, flower beds, fruit trees, an outdoor barbeque and even a swimming pool. They come in all shapes and sizes (Figs. 14-8 through 14-11).

Lawns are beautiful when well cared for, but the secret words are *cared for*. They usually need to be treated with fertilizer in the

Fig. 14-10. This adobe home includes a small patio.

Fig. 14-11. This small enclosed area serves as the patio for this adobe home.

spring and then have to be mowed throughout the summer in order to look nice. If you don't mind the job of repeated mowing, fine. Just be sure that the lawn mower can be stored nearby and doesn't have to be dragged across half of the house.

Flagstones make attractive sitting areas (Fig. 14-12). Place them loosely on the ground without the use of cement. Granted, weeds will spring up between them and will have to be pulled or cut. But when embedded in concrete, moisture has a way of seeping into the various cracks and during the next truly cold winter night it will freeze, expand and result in unsightly fissures.

Gravel walks tend to be more ornamental than practical. Gravel is commercially available in all colors, sizes and shapes. It looks nice but unless of a very small size, is not particularly pleasant to walk on (Fig. 14-13). Here too, weeds will have a tendency to grow through the gravel from the earth beneath. To avoid this you might want to consider covering the ground under the gravel with dark brown or black plastic sheets to effectively keep the weeds away. They should be carefully covered to the very edges because pieces of plastic may stick out here and there. They are quite ugly and will ruin the effect you've been after in the first place.

Shade trees provide shade in the summer but they shed their leaves in the fall, requiring constant raking of the ground for several

Fig. 14-12. This large walled patio is also covered with flagstone.

weeks. Fruit trees do the same and in addition they drop their fruit which, unless picked up, ends up rotting on the ground. All types of trees usually require dormant spraying in the early spring before the leaves start to bud in earnest. Otherwise they are likely to develop some kind of blight. In the higher elevations where below-freezing night temperatures are not at all unusual as late as early May, certain types of early blooming fruit trees, such as apricots, rarely bear fruit because their blossoms have been exposed to frost. Great apples are being grown in these same higher elevations in the Rocky Mountain states, but unless appropriately treated and sprayed, there is likely to be a worm in every apple. Also, birds just love to feast on the fruit just before it is ripe enough to be picked. Peaches also do fine in this climate, but again the birds may be the major beneficiaries unless you can figure out a way to keep them away.

When selecting patio furniture try to select the kind which is least affected by weather. Certain of the more expensive plastic and metal lounges, chairs and tables can be safely left outdoors in rain and snow. This is great because it becomes a bothersome chore to have to remove the outdoor furniture every time there is a change in the weather. Redwood is also weather resistant, but requires pillows and pads in order to be comfortable. Of course they will have to be protected from repeated exposure to moisture.

Fig. 14-13. A concrete covered walk leads to a patio area on the north side of the house and is easier to walk on than a gravel walkway.

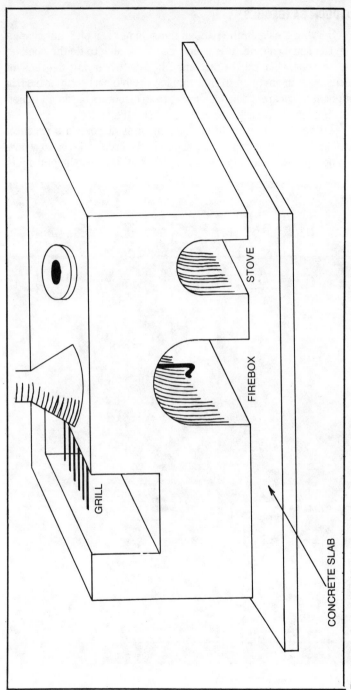

Fig. 14-14. An outdoor kitchen.

OUTDOOR BARBEQUES

Serving meals on the patio in the summer is a pleasant change from the usual routine. It is a nice idea to be able to do the cooking outside too. This can be accomplished with varying degrees of efficiency with anything from a simple portable barbeque or hibachi bought at the nearest discount store, to an elaborate outdoor kitchen built of adobe and including an oven, fireplace and stove.

To build such an outdoor kitchen, first decide on a practical location. It should form an integral part of the area of the patio where the appropriate tables and chairs are located. It is also helpful if it is

Fig. 14-15. A unique outdoor oven.

not so far from the house that all eating and cooking implements have to be carried long distances. Also consider the prevailing wind direction. An outdoor kitchen produces smoke and you wouldn't want to have to close every window on one side of the house to make sure that the house itself doesn't end up full of smoke.

Once the location has been decided upon, a concrete slab of about 5 or 6 by 15 or so feet should be poured. If the ground is firm and undisturbed it probably won't need any reinforcement or excessive thickness. It should be thick enough to minimize the chance of cracking and to safely carry the weight of the adobe structure which will be built on top of it.

While it is possible to use the top of the concrete slab as the base for the oven and fireplace, it is probably a better suggestion to place one or even two courses of adobe brick atop the slab. Recess it from the edge of the slab by about 1 to 1½ feet on one long side and less on the other three sides. This recess is needed to act as a hearth for the fireplace and oven (Fig. 14-14). The adobe courses make access to the fireplace and oven easier without having to always stoop all the way to the ground.

Then, on the left or right side of this base, adobe bricks are built up to a height of about 2½ feet into a solid structure which constitutes the base of the grill. It is then built up further on three sides, leaving sufficient space in the center for the grill. In the process of doing this, the iron grill rods are inserted at a sufficient height above the base to permit building a charcoal or wood fire underneath.

Adjoining this structure we build a beehive-type fireplace. This will not have to have the angled walls inside the firebox that are needed in interior fireplaces since we are not concerned with heating the patio. It also can probably safely eliminate the smoke baffle and damper. When building this structure entirely of adobe brick, hooks should be inserted which will permit hanging pots over the fire. The entire fireplace structure will take up little more than one-third of the overall outdoor kitchen unit.

Next to it an oven is built. Similar in construction to the fireplace, it will have a smaller opening in front. There is no chimney or flue (Fig. 14-15). We simply leave an opening at the top for which an appropriately sized metal cover must be obtained. A grill may be placed over that opening at the top which will permit hanging a chicken, or turkey or some such animal on a hook above the fire.

HORNOS

An alternate suggestion might be to forget about the oven and to build an authentic Indian *horno* on the third portion of the outdoor

Fig. 14-17. An Indian horno is used to bake bread.

kitchen (Figs. 14-16 through 14-20). A horno is a beehive-shaped enclosure used by the Indians to bake bread or to roast turkeys (Fig. 14-21). When baking bread a fire is built inside and left to burn until it is reduced to ashes, heating the horno itself to a high temperature. The ashes are then brushed out and the shaped bread dough is put inside. All openings, the larger front opening and the smoke hole are tightly closed and the bread bakes in the heat radiated inside by the hot adobe brick. If a turkey is to be baked, the coals are left in the

Fig. 14-18. An Indian horno can also be used to cook turkeys.

Fig. 14-16. Hornos are Indian ovens.

Fig. 14-19. Indian hornos can be found at the Taos and Santa Clara Pueblos in New Mexico.

oven and the turkey, on a metal pan, is placed on top of them. All openings are again tightly closed and the turkey is left to its own devices for several hours, cooking in its own juices.

To build a horno, adobe bricks have to be cut to the appropriate size. Or you might want to construct a special form and pour adobes of the size and shape needed. Once all of the bricks are in place, the inside can be left bare. The outside should be carefully plastered with

Fig. 14-20. Replicas of Indian hornos can be built in your own back yard.

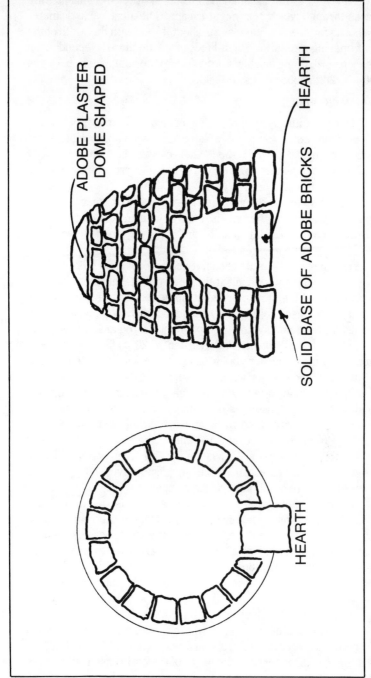

ADOBE PLASTER
DOME SHAPED

HEARTH

SOLID BASE OF ADOBE BRICKS

HEARTH

Fig. 14-21. Basic construction of a horno.

207

several layers of the usual adobe plaster in order to eliminate any cracks through which heat might escape. The ideal inside diameter of a horno for average home use is about 2 feet, with the width of the front opening measuring about 1 foot or a little more. Depending on the exact size of the finished horno, it will take somewhere between 100 and 200 adobe bricks to build.

SWIMMING POOLS

Once a status symbol of the super rich, swimming pools today are virtually taken for granted in regions where the winters are acceptably mild. Even in the higher elevations with their fairly severe winter weather for periods of five months, more and more pools are built each year.

A pool is a lovely thing to have regardless of whether you are an avid swimmer or whether you just like to take an occasional plunge. It is decorative, pleasant to sit by and gives an added dimension of elegance to outdoor entertaining.

Though never exactly cheap, it usually proves to be considerably less expensive when built at the same time as the house because excavating and the other needed equipment are already on the site and are being used to construct foundations and retaining walls.

Don't build an Olympic-size pool unless you are in training to compete in the Olympics. A dimension of 20 by 30 feet is about average. A much smaller pool tends to make it look like a displaced bathtub and much bigger will greatly increase the cost and problem of keeping it clean and heated. Though it requires in the neighborhood of 20,000 gallons of water to initially fill a pool, once filled the water is simply circulated through a system of filters and all that needs to be added from time to time is the amount lost through evaporation. A diving board is nice for the kids or anyone who likes to show off his or her expertise at executing fancy dives, but otherwise it would seem to be an unnecessary expense.

In areas where winter weather is of no consequence outdoor pools can be left filled and uncovered throughout the year. In such locations I have known of homes where the builder has extended a portion of the pool right into the house living room or even bedroom, providing a glass partition which can be lowered to just below the surface of the water to keep out wind or cold. This sounds like a lovely idea, but in practice I wouldn't be too surprised if it didn't prove to be more of a nuisance than it's worth.

Pools in parts of the country where severe winters are common do present some additional problems. In most cases they will have to be drained of all water with the onset of the cold season. What then remains is a relatively ugly hole in the ground into which small

Fig. 14-22. Equipped with a bubble enclosure, this pool can be used year around.

children or dogs may fall if no adequate protection is provided. The winds will blow large amounts of dust and dirt into it, resulting in a fairly unpleasant cleaning chore before it can be refilled in the spring.

One alternative is to install one of those plastic bubble-type pool enclosures which are kept inflated by a fan which blows heated air into the inside (Fig. 14-22). Thus equipped, the pool can be used year-round, no matter what the outside temperature is. The only real drawback is looks. Those pool enclosures tend to look like an incapacitated Goodyear blimp. The question which must be decided is whether your ability to use the pool for 12 months of the year is worth an oversized eyesore in your patio.

One word of warning. If you have small children, either teach them to swim as soon as they are old enough to crawl, or arrange for some sort of protection to keep them from falling into the pool. Each year we read about children who have drowned in pools. Make sure that it doesn't ever happen to yours.

Chapter 15
Utilities And Plumbing

The subjects briefly touched upon in this chapter are unglamorous and complicated, but necessary. Since all except the most experienced home builders will certainly want to have this work done by professionals, it seems unnecessary to go into great detail. For this reason we will simply provide what might best be described as a checklist.

HEATING

There are various ways in which you can heat your home. A few of the choices will be explained here.

Forced Air

Forced-air heating systems consist of a heater, ducts which carry the heated air to the various rooms in the house, additional ducts which draw air from the rooms back to the heater to be reheated, a fan to keep the air moving and two thermostats. The most efficient duct system brings the heated air into the rooms at the floor or baseboard level, while the return air is sucked out through openings near the ceiling. Since warm air rises to the ceiling, this results in less operation of the heater than would be required if the return air was pulled from the room at floor level.

One of the thermostats is located somewhere where the average room temperature can be expected, usually in a hallway. When the temperature at that location drops below that for which the thermostat is set, it activates the heater. The heater starts to heat the air and as soon as the air has reached a given temperature, a second thermostat, located in the duct system near the heater, causes the fan to start operating.

Ducts may be of a variety of material. Some can be embedded in earth without extra protection while others may have to be encased in concrete to avoid corrosion. In structures with basements or crawl spaces, the ducts can simply run beneath the house. Where there are no such spaces, they may have to be embedded in the earth or in the walls. Provisions must be made during the early process of constructing if this will be necessary.

Electric Heat

Electric heaters are usually laid along the floorboards. They look much like a floorboard with a narrow opening along the top. They require no special consideration in the construction of the house and they are clean, simple and quiet. However, it takes a little while to get a room heated to a comfortable temperature. They are also rather expensive in day-to-day operation, although in some areas utility companies offer reduced rates to homes heated with electricity. One of the advantages is the fact that each room can have its own thermostat, thus only the rooms actually in use need to be heated.

Hot-water Heaters

Hot-water heaters operate in two modes. One is referred to as radiant heat. It forces heated water through a system of thin, soft copper pipes which are set directly into the concrete slab or mud floor. This constitutes the base for the brick or tile used as the floor surface. This results in a very delightful even heating, but like electric heat, it also takes quite a while to heat a room to a comfortable temperature. On the other hand, once the floor surface has been adequately heated, it will retain that warmth for considerable periods of time. During cold winter months it might be desirable to include some type of time device which turns the heat on an hour or so before it's time to get up.

The other mode uses the heated water to operate radiators in the various rooms. Such radiator units are not particularly attractive, but can be dressed up to be less objectionable.

In either case, the various rooms can be equipped with individual thermostats which activate or deactivate separate water lines.

Fuel

The fuel used to operate the forced-air or water heaters can be natural gas, fuel oil, coal, LPG or electricity. Despite the huge increases in prices in recent years, natural gas is still the most convenient and probably least expensive in the long run if it is available in your area.

COOLING

Particularly in certain regions of the United States, cooling your house is vital to comfortable living. Some of the available options will be discussed now.

Cooling Through Evaporation

In areas with a low prevailing humidity level, evaporative cooling is practical, efficient and cheap. It consists of a unit usually mounted on the roof which contains sheets of some sort of absorbing material and a fan. Water is dripped slowly onto the absorbing sheets and the fan blows air across those sheets and into the house. As the water evaporates it cools the air and at the same time increases its moisture content.

Ideally the cooled air should enter the different rooms at some point near the ceiling, allowing it to descend within the room by its own weight. Each room so cooled must have some kind of ventilation. A slightly open door or window or the flue of a fireplace will permit air to escape and cooled air to continue to enter.

Air Conditioning

Standard air conditioning works on the same principle as the refrigerator, whether it uses gas or electricity. Circulating air is forced over a heat exchanger and then blown through a system of ducts into the various rooms. This type of air conditioning is usually unnecessary in the higher elevations where the air, even in the midst of summer, remains at a reasonable temperature regardless of the heat produced by the sun. In these regions the insulating quality of adobe will usually be sufficient to keep the house comfortably cool with the kind of ventilation afforded by opening windows.

On the other hand, in the low deserts such a cooling system becomes a virtual necessity if the house is to be livable during the summer heat.

Whether air conditioning or evaporative cooling is installed, it is usually possible to use the same system of ducts that serves the heating units during the winter.

213

ELECTRICITY

In order for the utility company to even consider hooking your house up to electrical service, the wiring, fuse boxes, switches, plugs and the like will have been inspected and approved. There are certain variations in the building codes with reference to electricity. Therefore, it is advisable to consult a licensed electrician before embarking on a do-it-yourself electrical installation.

In any case, be sure to include an ample number of outlets all over the house. There is nothing more obnoxious and potentially dangerous than to have a profusion of extension cords hanging around all over the place. Also remember that hallways and rooms which are habitually entered into at one end and left at the other require two-way switches in order to make it possible to turn the light on or off at either end. In rooms in which no ceiling light is provided, at least one of the wall plugs should be on a switch so that floor or table lamps can be turned on or off when entering or leaving the room.

GAS

Most gas companies will connect or disconnect gas appliances at no cost in order to make sure that such installations are performed by professionals and that there are no leaks.

PLUMBING

Like electrical conduit and gas lines, all plumbing must be planned in advance and incorporated into the basic structure of the house. The main water supply line leading into the average house should be at least ¾ inch in order to provide adequate water quantity and pressure. Pipes may be of copper, galvanized iron or, where building codes permit, plastic. Copper is more expensive than galvanized pipe, but it lasts longer. All metal-pipe installations require all manner of specialized tools, not to mention a fair degree of the knowledge of working with the tools and material. Hire a plumbing contractor. It's likely to be cheaper in the long run.

If your home is located within access to a city water system, you will most likely have no choice but to tie into that system and pay for the water being used. If your building project is way out in the boondocks, you may have to drill a well. Check around for a professional well driller who is familiar with the area because he will have a fair idea as to the best location in which to drill your well as well as the depth to which he may have to drill. He will not guarantee water at any given depth, but will charge you by the foot. This includes the cost of casings and such. The bid should also include a pressure tank of adequate size and the necessary pump. The size and power of the pump may depend on the depth from which the water must be pumped. Wells are not cheap, but once drilled the water is free forever except for the small amount of power used to operate the pump. With the prevailing cost of water in some areas these days, many homeowners are drilling their own wells despite the fact that access to a city water system is available.

Where there is water there has to be a sewer. Again, if a city sewer system is available, the logical thing is to hook into it. Where that is not possible a septic tank must be placed below ground at the appropriate level and hooked up to a seepage pit or leach field. Get professional advice to make sure that the septic tank does not contaminate the drinking water and that the seepage pit or leach field is located in an area where an excessive amount of plant growth does not interfere with the use of patio or garden areas.

Chapter 16
Remodeling An Old Adobe

So far we have talked and thought in terms of putting a brand-new structure onto an empty piece of ground. Now let's examine what is involved if you happen to find an old adobe with lots of charm that is located on a beautiful lot and you decide to buy and restore it (Fig. 16-1). At first glance this may seem to be quite a bit simpler than it will eventually turn out to be.

First of all you have to examine the old structure in order to determine whether or not it is worth remodeling. Many really old adobes were built on inadequate foundations such as rock without cement mortar. The simple fact that the walls are still standing is not necessarily proof that they will continue to do so.

If what you have found is the nearest thing to a ruin, no matter how charming it may look from the outside, it may prove to be the better part of valor to tear the whole thing down and start from scratch. You can save the still usable adobe bricks and wooden beams, latillas and vigas though. This decision should be based primarily on the soundness of the foundations and on the condition of the walls. If the foundation is of concrete and without noticeable cracks or of rocks embedded in concrete, again without any major cracks which would indicate that it has shifted in some distant past, then it is reasonably safe to assume that it will be capable of continuing to support the structure. This should include whatever is involved in the remodeling process.

Such an examination will probably necessitate a certain amount of digging around the foundation and the removal of large amounts of

Fig. 16-1. An old adobe is in the process of being remodeled. New lintels have been placed above window openings and new plaster applied overall. Note the huge abutment against the left wall. This may or may not contain a fireplace even though no chimney is evident.

dirt in order to get a good look at the foundation itself. Don't assume that just because one little corner looks fine, the rest will also be in satisfactory condition. Look at all of it. If there are only one or two cracks somewhere, it may be possible to dig a hole underneath and pour a new foundation under that portion of the old one which seems to be in doubt.

What is the condition of the walls? Has the plaster washed away and has run-off water started to affect the bricks and mortar? If so, it may still be salvageable if the wall is thick enough. A 10- or 14-inch wall which is starting to show serious signs of decay may not be worth salvaging. At best, it may require replacement in parts. Unless in really terrible shape a thicker wall using two adobes side-by-side of 20-, 24- or 28-inch thickness can probably be repaired.

The roof is likely to be in worse shape than anything else. Adobe roofs, particularly the kind traditionally used in building old adobes are certain to start to leak and gradually decay when left unattended for any length of time. In all probability the roof will have to be removed down to the vigas, decking or latillas and be com-

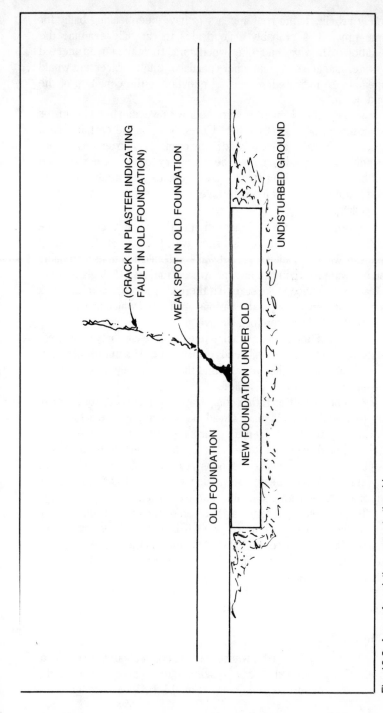

Fig. 16-2. A new foundation supports the old one.

pletely rebuilt. If the roof appears to have been leaking badly for some time, it is probably a good idea to carefully examine the condition of the vigas and other woodwork. Have they been affected by water damage to a point where partial or total replacement would appear to be indicated? A related question is the condition of the bond beam.

Many of the old adobes were built with wooden bond beams or without bond beams altogether. Unless you can be certain that a satisfactory bond beam was used in the original construction and that it is still in good condition, it will be necessary to remove not only the roof but also the ceiling structure in order to pour a new concrete bond beam that will then be strong enough to support the new roof and ceiling.

Another important consideration is the physical layout of the existing structure. Are you satisfied with the size and number of rooms or will you want to tear out walls and build additions? Probably you will want to put in bigger windows and maybe sliding glass doors to lead to the patio. Make sure that there is space to accommodate a modern kitchen and all of the various appliances which are a necessary part of today's comfortable living.

The condition of the plumbing must also be carefully examined. Rusted or leaking pipes will need replacement. As a matter of fact, it is not at all unlikely that you will find that an entirely new plumbing system will have to be installed.

Another and often rather complicated problem is the question of how to provide heat. In many old adobes the only source of heat was provided by the many fireplaces throughout the house. Cutting or buying enough wood to keep an entire house heated by means of fireplaces can be a nuisance, expensive or both. Some kind of more convenient means of heating the house will have to be added, but this can prove to be rather difficult in an old structure.

It is reasonably safe to say that remodeling an old adobe, even one in acceptable condition, will prove to be not much less expensive than building a new one. Still, if the location and the usable portion of the old structure are of sufficient appeal, it can be a worthwhile and satisfying undertaking.

Let's look at some of the basic specifics involved in adapting an existing structure to your needs.

FOUNDATIONS

As stated previously, where there is doubt about the solidity of an existing foundation, excavate beneath it and pour a new foundation to add support to the old one (Fig. 16-2). When adding to the

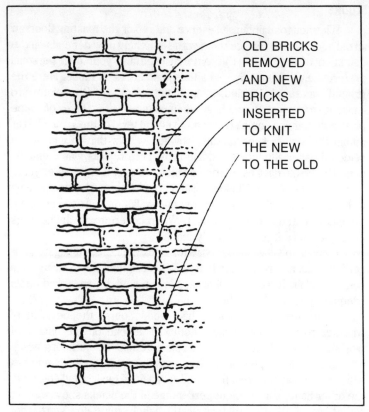

OLD BRICKS
REMOVED
AND NEW
BRICKS
INSERTED
TO KNIT
THE NEW
TO THE OLD

Fig. 16-3. Integrating a new wall into the old one.

house, pour the foundation for the addition down to a low enough level so that it extends under the old foundation for at least a foot or so. It can then be built up with a higher stem to the future level of the flooring. While you're at it, decide if you want any additional fireplaces. If so, pour those foundations to the appropriate size and thickness and include reinforcement with rebars at the same time.

WALLS

Where a portion of a wall will have to be rebuilt or where a new wall is to abut against an old one, the replacement will have to be integrated into the old structure (Fig. 16-3). To do this, remove some of the old bricks in alternating courses, scraping away the old mortar and loose dirt and then fit new bricks into those spaces with new mortar. This combines the new and the old into an integral whole.

FLOORS

Whether to maintain, preserve and repair the existing floors in an old adobe, or to replace them with something new depends on the condition of the floors, the material used and your own personal preference. Traditionally, old adobes had floors of adobe. Here the ground was simply leveled, tamped and sprinkled with moisture to cause it to harden. It may have been covered with a layer of adobe plaster containing some straw and a second level of the same plaster minus the straw, subsequently washed with a thin mix of adobe selected especially for its reddish-brown color. This was then hardened in the old days by pouring ox blood all over it and in later years with mixtures of boiled linseed oil and turpentine. Such a floor seems to have a carpet-like texture when one walks on it. It can be damp mopped, dusted and even waxed. When covered with Indian rugs here and there it is very lovely indeed.

It can also serve as the base for brick floors, but if flagstone or ceramic tile are to be used, it will necessitate the pouring of a concrete slab. In very small areas tile can sometimes be laid on an adequately tamped mud floor.

If the original old adobe had wood floors, the decision of whether to repair or replace them will depend on the quality of workmanship and the degree of deterioration. Wood floors which have been walked upon for generations will have a certain unevenness which is quite attractive if the wood is of a good quality and color. On the other hand, if a sufficient percentage of the planks show signs of rot, it may be better to tear up the whole thing and start from scratch.

DOORS AND WINDOWS

Assuming the lintel above a window opening is in good condition, the size of the window can be increased downward or it can be turned into a door without any structural problems. All that needs to be done is to remove the old window frame, cut out the adobes below, remove some adobe mortar where new nailing blocks are needed and then install the frame for the new window or door.

To install a new window where none existed previously or to widen a window or door will involve a degree of structural precaution. With no existing lintel to carry the weight of the roof, or in the case of widening an existing opening, the fact that the old lintel has to be removed and replaced means that supports have to be provided to carry that weight until a new lintel has been put in place. The simplest way of doing this is to cut wooden beams to the length which

222

Fig. 16-4. Small, permanently closed windows set directly into the thick adobe wall can add charm to your home.

equals the distance from the floor to the bottom of the vigas. These beams are then wedged vertically between the floor and each of the vigas which lie atop the part of the wall where the opening is to be cut or enlarged.

With these supports in place, the hole can then be cut into the wall or the old lintel removed and the opening enlarged as desired. At the top of the opening a recess of at least 1 foot on each side must be provided to receive the new or larger lintel. Once that new lintel is firmly in place and secured, it will carry the weight of the roof. The temporary supports can then be removed.

Sometimes it is desirable to have some small, permanently closed windows to bring light into a dark hall or corner of a room. If they are small enough and are not located directly under a viga, an opening for them can be cut safely without installing any temporary supports. Such a window will require only a minimum lintel and no other framing at all. Simply place the glass into the opening and plaster around it with adobe plaster. By shaping the plaster accordingly, you can produce any shape window that might seem attractive in that particular place. It can be round, oval, rectangular with rounded corners, L-shaped, T-shaped, triangular or whatever turns you on (Figs. 16-4 and 16-5).

CEILINGS

Unless the roof is a total disaster, the ceiling in an old adobe is likely to be in pretty good shape and one of its most beautiful features. It is therefore important that if additions are built, the new ceilings blend in with the old. It is somehow disconcerting to have one part of the house with ceilings of vigas and latillas and the new part with plain plaster ceilings. By matching the style to the greatest degree possible, the house will present a feeling of unity rather than one consisting of two portions: one old and the other new.

ROOFS

Assuming that the roof of the old adobe is in good enough shape to be retained and repaired where needed, certain considerations must be kept in mind when planning additions. Which way does the water run off? If the addition is on the side of the run-off, the new roof must be at the right level and correctly slanted to permit the water to run off across it. In that case the old coping may have to be removed. Otherwise the water will run in narrow streams across the new roof, increasing the likelihood of eventual damage.

Fig. 16-5. Permanently closed windows can be any shape you like.

Fig. 16-6. Where a bearing wall is to be removed, some alternate means of support may have to be installed.

Fig. 16-7. A decorative vertical beam may be used to support part of the ceiling and roof.

227

If the addition is not on the run-off side, the old coping can be left in place. But then the new roof must be slanted in a different direction to assure run-off away from the coping.

REMOVING WALLS

Many of the older adobes consist of many small rooms, several of which may be profitably combined into fewer but larger ones. This would involve the removal of interior walls. The first determination which has to be made is to make sure that the wall in question is not a bearing wall. Check the vigas. If it is obvious that the vigas on both sides of the wall are one and the same and that they extend from one bearing wall to another bearing wall through the top of the non-bearing wall that is to be removed, then it is safe to assume that the wall can be knocked away without impairing the structural solidity of the house as a whole.

That having been determined, decide whether you want to knock out all of the wall or whether it might be attractive to maintain a short section of it as a partial partition and a decorative corner on either side. If there is a fireplace in one of those corners or if you have decided that you would like to install a fireplace there, then it goes without saying that a short section of the wall will have to be maintained. Such a short partition or *padercita* (little wall) need not rise straight up to the ceiling. It is more attractive to recess it in regular or irregular steps, thus reducing its length as it rises up.

In removing all or part of a wall, it will pay to do the work slowly, removing one brick at a time. Some will certainly break or crumble, but a large number can be salvaged and stored for later use elsewhere. Doing it that way also helps to not accidentally damage electrical conduit or gas lines which might have been built into the wall. Where such lines are discovered they will, of course, have to be removed and their ends secured to be certain that there is no danger of electrical short circuits or gas leakage.

If the interior wall that is to be removed runs parallel to the direction of the vigas, it is safe to assume that it is not supporting any weight. But if there is any doubt, it might be a good idea to ask a professional, either a builder or an architect, to take a look at it. After all, you don't want to take a chance of having the whole place collapse around your ears.

If all or part of a bearing wall is to be removed, precautions will have to be taken to install some other means of supporting the weight of the ceiling and the roof (Fig. 16-6). In that case vertical beams will have to be inserted under each of the vigas on each side of the wall for the entire distance to which the wall is to be knocked out. With these supports in place, the obsolete portion of the wall can

Fig. 16-8. Attractive and decorative buttresses built against an old patio wall provide strength.

then be removed. Recesses will have to be cut into the tops of the parts of the wall to be retained and a lintel of the appropriate size and strength must be inserted. It must be large enough to safely support the ends of the vigas on both sides of the former wall. If the opening is really wide, say 15 or more feet, it might be advisable to place an attractive vertical beam under the center of the crossbeam as a permanent additional support (Fig. 16-7).

If such a wall is equipped with a sturdy bond beam, it might be advisable and attractive to retain that bond beam and possibly one or several courses of adobe brick beneath it and insert the crossbeam below. There should still be adequate height to permit people to walk without hitting their heads. It will also help to screen the fact that the vigas on either side of the wall are not in the identical position.

REPAIRING EXTERIOR WALLS

Frequently exterior walls show cracks in places where the foundation has weakened. Aside from strengthening the foundation by pouring a new section of foundation under the weakened portion of the old one, the wall itself will need repair and possibly some strengthening. If the crack is simply in the plaster and does not extend to the brick portion of the wall itself, it can simply be replastered because the new foundation should inhibit any further movement of the wall. On the other hand, if the wall itself is cracked, it will require more extensive reworking.

If the crack happens to be in a place where you would like to install a window or door, a new lintel can serve to hold the wall together. If the wall is to remain solid or if a major portion of the crack remains above or below the new window or above the new door, then a sufficient number of the old bricks may have to be removed to permit inserting new bricks with new mortar. This may be done safely by removing only a small section at a time, repairing it and then removing the next section.

In cases where the wall has been seriously weakened, a buttress can be erected against the wall on the outside. This is a frequently used means of supporting the walls of old adobes. It can be rather attractive when it becomes an integral feature of the overall adobe structure (Fig. 16-8).

REINFORCING OLD FOUNDATIONS

Aside from adding new sections of foundation under weak spots of the old one, it is frequently necessary to protect the base of the wall where it meets the foundation from continued water damage. To do this a narrow concrete foundation reinforcement should be run along the outside of the old foundation and the base of the wall. To accomplish this a trench must be dug around the entire outside of the house down to below the frost line. This trench will serve as a form for the newly poured cement, but a wooden form will have to be built to a height of about 1 foot so that the newly poured foundation reinforcement will rise to about that distance above ground level. Once the cement is poured but is still workable, it should be finished on top as a beveled ledge, slanting outward to permit rainwater and melting snow to run off away from the wall. Be sure that there are no cracks between this new foundation and the wall itself where water might collect and seep into the wall or freeze and cause damage.

Chapter 17
Solar Adobe

By far the largest number of adobe structures, both old and new, can be found in areas with a relatively arid climate. In other words, they are found in areas with an above-average amount of sunshine. It is therefore not surprising that in recent years much has been done to combine adobe building and solar heating.

Architects and builders involved in solar construction are constantly experimenting with new ideas, but basically there are two methods of using the energy of the sun: active and passive.

SOLAR COLLECTORS

An active system uses *solar collectors* (Figs. 17-1 and 17-2). They are flat boxes covered with a sheet of glass and black painted metal sheets above about 4 or 5 inches of air space. Inside these panels the air heats quickly to about 170 degrees Fahrenheit. It is then forced by a system of ducts and fans toward a material which will absorb and maintain this heat. This can be a space under the house filled with large-size gravel contained in some sort of chicken-wire enclosure or it can be a fairly large body of water, such as a storage tank or even a swimming pool.

When gravel is used for heat storage, the room where it is stored (usually a cellar below the floor level of the house) will become quite hot and the hot air can be circulated throughout the house in the same manner used in standard forced-air heating systems. Experience seems to indicate that a solar-collector surface of approximately one-third of the square footage of the dwelling is

Fig. 17-1. Solar collector panels apparently added after the house was built.

required in order to produce sufficient warmth to keep it at a comfortable level for several sunless days during even the coldest winter.

Figure 17-3 is an active solar dwelling, built of adobe, but with little regard to what is generally referred to as adobe style. It uses 28 solar collector panels on the south slope of the roof, pumping the hot air into a heat storage area underneath the house and then distributing that heat to the various rooms in the house in the usual forced-air heating manner. This house is located in the Arroyo Hondo area near Santa Fe. Its owner says that the heating remains effective for three to four sunless days, even during the coldest winter months.

The picture in Fig. 17-4 was taken in the basement where a large area, encircled by steel posts and wire mesh, contains large gravel piled about 4 feet high. On sunny days the hot air from the solar collector panels is forced into the gravel, raising the temperature to 150 or more degrees.

If the heat generated by the solar collectors is used to heat water in a storage tank, this heated water must then be circulated to water radiators throughout the house (Fig. 17-5). By far the most comfortable, but also expensive, means of using water to heat the house is to embed water lines in the floor base beneath brick, tile or flagstone floors. It results in a slow warming which rises evenly from all portions of the floor. The floor itself will retain a degree of warmth for some time even when the water begins to cool. In houses with

Fig. 17-2 Solar collector panels have been installed on the roof of a conventional adobe home.

Fig. 17-3. An active solar dwelling.

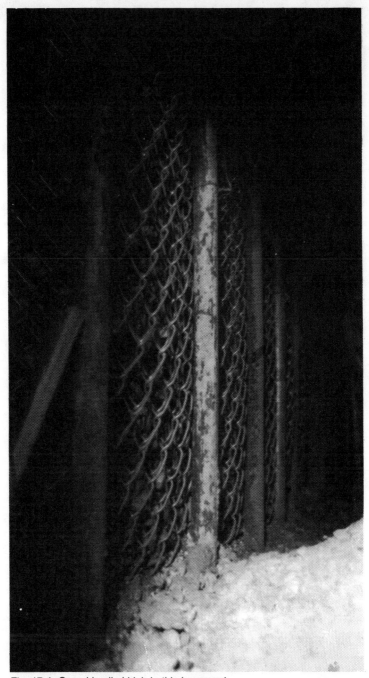

Fig. 17-4. Gravel is piled high in this basement.

Fig. 17-5. A solar collector panel, placed against a workshop building in the back yard, is being tested to see if it will suffice to produce the needed amount of hot water. The hot air which collects in the panel is being sucked through the circular duct by the fan which can be seen in the extreme foreground. It is then forced on to its destination.

wood floors or where for some other reason this type of heating is not practical, regular water radiators can be installed.

Heating a swimming pool in this manner and using its water to circulate through the heating system in the house would not seem practical. A swimming pool has a huge surface exposed to the cold air outside and would tend to cool too fast to be effective. If covered by a heated enclosure, its water would probably become too warm to be used for a refreshing swim.

Fig. 17-6. A passive solar home.

237

Fig. 17-7. A passive solar-heated home in the final stages of construction.

PASSIVE SOLAR HOMES

Passing solar homes operate on a different principle (Fig. 17-6). In such houses large window areas are installed to catch the rays of the sun, usually faced inside by massive walls of adobe or some other heat-absorbent material. The walls should be painted a dark color to maximize absorption and minimize reflection. The sun hits these walls and warms them sufficiently to give off heat for considerable periods of time after the sun has set. This type of heating is not sufficient to spread throughout an entire house, however. Therefore each room not facing the sun must be equipped with appropriately placed skylights through which the rays of the sun can shine and warm a given portion of the opposite wall.

When using this passive system, care must be taken to provide for ventilation and a means of reducing the effect of the sun's heat. Otherwise they will become virtual hot boxes during the summer.

In Fig. 17-7 a passive solar-heated home is in the final stages of construction atop one of the higher hills around Santa Fe. Built into the side of the natural rock in a manner similar to that used by the cliff-dwelling Indians long ago, it will use the heat-absorbing capability of the natural rock to store solar warmth for cold nights and sunless days.

The southside of the house, constructed of concrete blocks with adobe supports (far right of Fig. 17-8) includes a greenhouse covered by glass panes. The rays of the sun heat the concrete-block wall beyond it, transferring the warmth to the interior. Louvres at top and bottom can be opened during the summer to avoid excessive heat.

The flat roof of Fig. 17-9 is speckled with skylights, one for practically every room. These skylights are placed in such a manner that the sun will hit an interior wall which is designed to absorb the warmth and retain it throughout the night and to some extent a sunless day. The rays of the sun shining in through a sky light, light and warm a thick interior wall constructed of natural rock (Fig. 17-10). This will retain the warmth for a considerable length of time. Also built into the wall is a fireplace which will be used to heat the room if the sun should fail to shine for several days in a row.

GREENHOUSE SYSTEM

A variation on this system is the so-called *greenhouse*. Patios, balconies, verandahs or other areas on the south side of the house may be enclosed with glass or clear plastic. This will form a kind of storage space for the sun-heated air which can then be funneled into

Fig. 17-8. A greenhouse covered by glass panes is being included in the construction of this solar adobe home.

Fig. 17-9. This flat roof is speckled with skylights.

the house. If glass is used in a permanent installation, means must be included to either remove the panes of glass or to open sections of it during the summer. Otherwise the heat would become unbearable. On the other hand, plastic can simply be used during the winter and then removed and thrown away. Plastic to enclose even a fairly large area would cost no more than maybe $20 or $30. Though cheap and efficient, it is not particularly attractive and may be impractical in a location where frequent strong winds may cause it to tear.

In Fig. 17-11 a framework has been constructed for a greenhouse. It will face south-westerly. When finished it can be covered with glass or clear plastic, thus serving during the winter as an additional source of solar warmth. At the same time it will provide a windbreak for the door leading to the patio.

As just mentioned, plastic is cheap and can be thrown away in the spring. Glass, on the other hand, is permanent. But it does require ample means of ventilation, either through the use of louvres or removable panels, This will avoid excessive heat during the summer months.

In Figs. 17-12 and 17-13 a glass-enclosed area on the south side of the house serves as the casual dining area and plant room. The

Fig. 17-10. The rays of the sun light warm a thick interior wall constructed of natural rock.

Fig. 17-11. A framework has been constructed for a greenhouse.

thick adobe walls are painted dark brown and absorb the warmth of the sun, keeping the house comfortable long after the sun has set.

SOLAR HOME COSTS

While the idea of solar heating sounds awfully nice, it does have its drawbacks. Solar collector panels and greenhouses, both of which can usually be installed on existing structures not originally designed for solar heating, tend to be unsightly. There is really no good way to hide them from view because they need to have an unobstructed exposure to the sun. Passive solar homes, on the other hand, must be designed and built as such from the start. The huge expanses of glass often result in a less than harmonious appearance however, especially when used in adobe structures which according to tradition call for smaller window areas.

The cost of building a solar home is still relatively high, usually some 10 per cent more than a conventional home. On the other hand, the cost of heating fuel has risen to such an extent during recent years that the average monthly heating bill for an average-sized house tends to exceed $100. This makes the potential savings offered by solar energy meaningful. In addition some states, includ-

Fig. 17-12. This glass-enclosed area serves as the casual dining area and plant room.

Fig. 17-13. By enclosing a glass balcony with a southern exposure, a greenhouse effect is being created. It then produces heat for the home.

ing New Mexico, offer tax rebates or deductions to people building solar homes or solar commercial structures.

It should be emphasized here that designing and building an efficient solar home, whether adobe or some other type, is a job for experienced experts. No one who has not studied its characteristics, advantages and limitations should undertake such a task without the help and advice from an architect or builder who has been involved with the subject for some time.

Glossary

adobe: A term said to have been derived from either the Spanish (*adobar* = plaster) or the Arabic (*at - tub* = brick) or the Coptic (*tobe* = brick). In modern usage is stands for the mud mixture used in adobe building, for the bricks made of adobe mud and for the structures built of adobe.

adobe brick: Bricks made of adobe mud, sand and straw that are dried in the sun.

adobe plaster: Mortar made of the same material and used for exterior and interior plaster of adobe-brick walls.

arroyo: A creek bed, usually dry most of the year except during the spring runoff.

asphalt roofing felt: A felt-like material impregnated with asphalt and used in the form of shingles or sheets in the construction of roofs.

bath, full: A bathroom consisting of a tub with or without shower, sink and toilet.

bath, half: A bathroom featuring only a sink and toilet.

bath, three-quarters: A bathroom with a stall shower, sink and toilet.

bearing wall: A wall which supports a portion of the ceiling and roof.

bond beam: A beam of concrete or wood, laid across the top of bearing walls to support the vigas or roof beams.

buttress: A solid adobe protrusion built onto the outside of adobe walls to improve their strength.

canale: An open drain, U-shaped in cross section. Its purpose is to drain the water off of the flat roofs of adobe structures.

cliff dwelling: Adobe-brick structures built against and into the vertical sides of cliffs by the Pueblo Indians in order to be more easily defended against hostile nomadic Indian tribes and the invading white man.

coping: An extension of the bearing walls above the upper surface of the roof, usually approximately 1 foot high. Canales are placed through holes in the coping to allow water run-off.

corbelled: An expression used for the type of brick construction, usually employed in the building of fireplaces where each brick sticks out a certain distance beyond the one below it.

course: A row of adobe bricks.

covenant: A contract between two or more persons. In real estate, a covenant usually implies some type of legal restriction or entanglement.

curtain walls: Thin nonbearing interior walls constructed of wooden studs and plasterboard.

damper: A means of shutting off the flue of a fireplace. It is located in the fireplace throat.

decking: The ceiling material placed atop the vigas or ceiling beams.

dormant spraying: The spraying of trees and shrubs with insecticide in the early spring before they start to bud.

easement: The right of utility companies and others to encroach upon a lot for the purpose of constructing power lines or to provide access to an otherwise inaccessible area.

face: The decorative outer surface of a fireplace.

fill: Earth piled into a hole or depression. Foundations may not be built on top of fill, but must sit on undisturbed ground.

firebox: The portion of a fireplace in which the fire is set.

fire brick: A special type of brick appropriate for use in the construction of fireplaces.

fire clay: A clay mortar used in fireplace construction.

flue: The inside of the chimney.

footing: Foundation.

gringo block: A wooden block approximately equal to the dimension of an adobe brick. It is inserted into the wall to permit nailing.

guy wires: Wires attached at an angle to a vertical post or beam to keep it in position.

hearth: A platform in front of a firebox, made of masonry or other nonflammable material and designed to catch ashes and cinders.

hibachi: A small portable grill in which charcoal is burned.

horno: A beehive-shaped Indian oven, used for baking bread or cooking turkeys.

joist: A wooden support for floor coverings.

kiva: A circular ceremonial chamber, built by the Peublo Indians either above or below ground. It is used primarily for religious ceremonies.

latilla: Thin wooden stakes, usually aspen or cedar, which are placed across the vigas to provide the ceiling and the base for the roof.

leach field: A system of perforated pipes layed below ground. The sewage flows from the septic tank into the leach field which permits it to soak into the ground.

lintel: A beam above a door or window opening, designed to support the weight of the wall and roof above that opening. It is usually wood.

LPG: Liquefied petroleum gas, stored in tanks and used in areas where access to natural gas is unavailable.

masonry: Construction of brick, stone, concrete, or a combination thereof. Adobe walls are considered masonry.

mezzanine: An indoor balcony or platform located above the main floor but below the second story.

mortar: In adobe building the adobe mud which is spread between the courses of adobe brick to hold them firmly together.

mud: A term frequently used with reference to adobe.

multiple dwelling: A dwelling designed to house more than one family.

nailing block: A piece of wood of any dimension inserted into an adobe wall to permit nailing.

padercita: Literally meaning little wall. The term applies to partial walls, usually constructed in order to permit locating a corner

247

fireplace in a room where the use of an actual corner is impractical.

parapet: Coping.

partition walls: Curtain walls.

patio-type brick: Nonporous brick used in the construction of brick floors and brick walks. Also known as *solids*.

plumb line: A line with a lead weight at one end, used to make sure that a wall or post is perfectly vertical.

pueblo: Communal building or group of buildings used by the Indians in the southwestern United States.

Pueblo Indian: The term applied by the Spaniards to the Anasazi Indians who lived (and still live) in permanent communities.

rebar: A steel reinforcing bar embedded in concrete construction to add strength.

refractory cement: Cement which is resistant to great heat.

retaining wall: A wall built to prevent the soil at an embankment or cut from sliding.

seepage pit: An underground pit designed to perform the same function as a leach field.

septic tank: A tank in which sewage decomposes before it is permitted to seep into the ground.

shell: The masonry enclosure of a fireplace which must be of adequate thickness to protect wood or other flammable materials located nearby.

shim: A block of wood or other material designed to keep vigas in place.

smoke shelf: A recessed portion in a fireplace designed to prevent downdrafts from blowing ashes and cinders into the room.

solids: See patio-type bricks.

spanish tile: Curved clay tile used in the construction of gabled roofs.

stem: A portion of the wall between the foundation and the actual adobe wall. Constructed of concrete blocks, it prevents water from damaging the adobe. Also the concrete-block base of a fireplace.

subfloor: A floor, usually of plywood, placed below the actual hardwood floor.

template: A pattern of wood or other material used as a guide in building given shapes.

territorial style: An adobe building style recognizable by the intricate brick design around the coping.

throat: The part of a fireplace between the smoke shelf and the flue.

toenailing: Nailing at an angle through two pieces of wood.

tongue-in-groove: Boards with a protrusion along one side and a matching indentation on the other. When placed together they result in a tight fit.

undisturbed ground: Firm ground with no fill. All foundation trenches must be excavated down to undisturbed ground.

vigas: Straight round tree trunks with all bark and branches removed and used as ceiling beams.

winch: A system of pulleys which permits hoisting heavy weights with a minimum of power.

Additional Reading

ABCs of Making Adobe Bricks. New Mexico State University, Las Cruces; Cooperative Extension Circular 429.

Adobe and Rammed Earth. United Nations, Housing and Town and Country Planning Bulletin #4.

Adobe Architecture. Myrtle Stedman; Sunstone Press.

Adobe Book. John F. O'Connor; Ancient City Press.

Adobe—Build it Youself. Paul Graham McHenry; University of Arizona Press.

Adobe Construction Methods. L. W. Neubauer; University of California, Agricultural Experiment Station, Extension Service.

Adobe Fireplaces. Myrtle Stedman; Sunstone Press.

Adobe News. Bi-monthly publication; P. O. Box 702, Las Lunas, New Mexico 87031.

Adobe or Sundried Brick for Farm Buildings. U.S. Department of Agriculture, Farmer's Bulletin #1720.

Adobe—Past and Present. William Lumpkins; Museum of New Mexico; Case-Thompson Printing Company.

Adobe Remodeling. Myrtle Stedman; Sunstone Press.

A Qualitative Comparison of Rammed Earth and Sundried Adobe Brick. University of New Mexico Press.

Build with Adobe. Marcia Southwick; Sage Books.

Build Your Own Adobe. Paul and Doris Aller; Stanford University.

Earthen Home Construction. A & M College of Texas, Texas Transportation Institute, Bulletin #18.

Handbook for Building Homes of Earth. U. S. Department of Housing and Urban Development, Division of International Affairs.

Making the Adobe Brick. Eugene H. Boudreau; Fifth Street Press.

Mud, Space and Spirit, Virginia Gray, Alan Macrae and Wayne McCall; Capra Press.

New Mexico Home Plan Book. George Fitzpatrick; Rydal Press.

Taos Adobes. Bainbridge Bunting; Museum of New Mexico Press.

The Manufacture of Asphalt Emulsion Stabilized Soil Bricks. International Institute of Housing Technology.

Index